POLLEN ARIA

POLLEN ARIA

CLAYTON ESHLEMAN

BLACK
WIDOW
PRESS

BOSTON

Black Widow Press is an imprint of Commonwealth Books, Inc., Boston, MA. Distributed to the trade by NBN (National Book Network) throughout North America, Canada, and the U.K. All Black Widow Press books are printed on acid-free paper, and glued into bindings. Black Widow Press and its logo are registered trademarks of Commonwealth Books, Inc.

Joseph S. Phillips and Susan J. Wood, Ph.D., Publishers
www.blackwidowpress.com

Cover Artwork: The Poet by William Paden, oil on canvas
Cover Design and Book Production: Kerrie L. Kemperman

ISBN-13: 978-0-9995803-9-4

Printed in the United States
10 9 8 7 6 5 4 3 2 1

ACKNOWLEDGEMENTS

Some of these poems and the Irakli Qolbaia Interview appeared, occasionally, in earlier forms, in the following periodicals & blogs: Rothenberg's *Poems & Poetics*, Joris' *A Nomad Poetics Revisited*, *The Dooris*, *Seedlings*, *Brooklyn Rail*, *x-peri*, *Dispatches from The Poetry Wars*, & *Rascal*.

Orphic Ontologies was published as a small chapbook by Estepha Editions in Paris, 2015.

Hybrid Hierophanies was published as a chapbook by BlazeVOX in 2016.

A longer version of *Sweetheart* was published by Canopic in Ypsilanti in 2002.

ALSO BY CLAYTON ESHLEMAN

POETRY

Mexico & North [1962]

Indiana [1969]

Altars [1971]

Coils [1973]

The Gull Wall [1975]

What She Means [1978]

Hades in Manganese [1981]

Fracture [1983]

The Name Encanyoned River: Se-
lected Poems 1960–1985 [1986]

Hotel Cro-Magnon [1989]

Under World Arrest [1994]

From Scratch [1998]

My Devotion [2004]

An Alchemist with One Eye
on Fire [2006]

Reciprocal Distillations [2007]

The Grindstone of Rapport [2008]

An Anatomy of the Night [2011]

Clayton Eshleman / The Essential
Poetry 1960–2015 [2015]

Penetralia [2017]

PROSE

Antiphonal Swing: Selected Prose
1962–1987 [1989]

Companion Spider: Essays [2002]

Juniper Fuse: Upper Paleolithic
Imagination & the Construction
of the Underworld [2003]

Archaic Design [2007]

The Price of Experience [2013]

JOURNALS AND ANTHOLOGIES

Folio [Bloomington, Indiana, 3
issues, 1959–1960]

Quena [Lima, Peru, 1 issue,
edited, then suppressed by the
North American Peruvian
Cultural Institute, 1966]

Caterpillar [New York–Los
Angeles, 20 issues, 1967–1973]

A Caterpillar Anthology [1971]

Sulfur [Pasadena–Los Angeles–
Ypsilanti, 46 issues, 1981–
2000]

A Sulfur Anthology [2015]

TRANSLATIONS

Pablo Neruda, *Residence on Earth* [1962]

César Vallejo, *The Complete Posthumous Poetry* (with José Rubia Barcia) [1978]

Aimé Césaire, *The Collected Poetry* (with Annette Smith) [1983]

Michel Deguy, *Given Giving* [1984]

Bernard Bador, *Sea Urchin Harakiri* [1986]

Conductors of the Pit: Major Works by Rimbaud, Vallejo, Césaire, Artaud, & Holan [1988, 2005]

Aimé Césaire, *Lyric & Narrative Poetry 1946–1982* (with Annette Smith) [1990]

César Vallejo, *Trilce* [1992, 2000]

Antonin Artaud, *Watchfiends & Rack Screams* (with Bernard Bador) [1995]

Aimé Césaire, *Notebook of a Return to the Native Land* (with Annette Smith) [2001]

César Vallejo, *The Complete Poetry* [2007]

Bernard Bador, *Curdled Skulls* [2010]

Bei Dao, *Endure* (with Lucas Klein) [2011]

Aimé Césaire, *Solar Throat Slashed* (with A. James Arnold) [2011]

Aimé Césaire, *The Original 1939 Notebook of a Return to the Native Land* (with A. James Arnold) [2013]

José Antonio Mazzotti, *Sakra Boccata* [2013]

The Complete Poetry of Aimé Césaire (with A. James Arnold) [2017]

BOOKS ON CLAYTON ESHLEMAN

Minding the Underworld: Clayton Eshleman & Late Postmodernism, Paul Christensen [1991]

Clayton Eshleman / The Whole Art, Edited by Stuart Kendall [2014]

TABLE OF CONTENTS

TO THE MUSE

Are you the spume of Laussel, archaic dust dimpled & savory?
Something in the air I nourish to steel myself against
the Selfhood that lays claim to all rapture?
And if Laussel—is it the poet she is raising in her right hand?
The eagle of inspiration sinks talons into our shoulders
lifting us up & off in flight to an underworld
echoing the Paleolithic as well as vaults in the Congo today,
monstrous deformations of psychic space.
So, I am held here in the grip of these printless digits
slightly above the head of one whose glacial face is scraped
clean of green immersions. Do I channel you through
the skull racks & roses assembled in Tenochtitlan & blessed by Dante
in a Beatricious swoon? Of what does inspiration consist?
Spires of incest over the ages, wirings
short-circuited, then re-fused. I suppose you are part pedestal
part sty part abyss part snake. And if I tunnel,
does the mud around me contain a cast of *yous,* cell walls, cloisters,
every woman with whom I have traded eyes, particles of
a nebula, all colors, gaseous edges, inner space?
You is your target, your mandala,
bison gaze through the puberty glyphs of transpersonal alarm,
you blank egg, rank ocelot aprowl in legends which enter me through
the godspell of *you.* The muse as *you,*
Pandora hexagram milling with changes,
ochre disk on a stone wall bearing in its menstrual, apotropaic sigil
the print of Cro-Magnon woman embedded so
deep in collective mind we can only wonder
if planetary peril is not inscribed from image's beginning.
And what might that script be? Palmed stone or horn fragment

felt as the presence of one dead, one dead as oneself,
oneself at a womb moment when preconsciousness percolated as
mother consciousness through the caul. Does
Laussel raise the supreme, spectral memory of this sensation?
You-image with its angel-insectile feelers
probing the jargon of consciousness to be
rising like a jellyfish drawn up through surging salt by
solar warmth. *You* muse, *you* image muzzle, *you* diaphanous mouth,
tasting the angel matter that I offer at the peak of Tenochtitlan
whose every level raised me closer to mortal closure.

7 January 2010

CLAYTON ESHLEMAN

STUDY FOR A PORTRAIT OF BETTY BRODY &
DAVID BERKOWITZ

The murderer's mother. In what elevator does she dwell?
Can my male hand reach the puncture moment in which she knew?
How much of this was her fault? Then, as a time, is so strong,
he becomes a child again, as if to shield her from the imagined face
through which his victims burn,
as if her home were the lobby of their crematorium.

Alone in the bathtub, there was a small of anima,
a sour bear belly Venus murk—something rutting on & on in the
    male mind,
a senseless piston pumping, oblivious to its turbined mass.
As if a single form were responsible for the male plight,
a pretty girl's skirt sawed by breeze,
buttocks full of cleave & fault,
a swamp, endless, he feels, in which a gold cross ceaselessly
impregnates self. "I am deeply hurt by your calling me a wemon
    hater.
I am not. But I am a monster. I am 'Son of Sam.'"

How powerfully this chain of archetypal screens is set,
like a stacked deck in the woman killer's mind.
He is shuffled every time another man appears
as if around that guy corner is someone like The Old Maid,
with muzzle, bending over his crib.
She has warm, brown eyes, she brings him an egg.
He cannot stand the way her sympathy corridors into a spine
that does not idealize him, or the way her disappearance does not
prepare him for an unknown father's jaw.

If only he could wringer her out of his flesh,

would he not then be slender & handsome?

But her loss looks out of his eyes into eyes he believes will reject him.

The world has sets of eyes, like teeth, sewn into the rock of love.

1979   Written on the flyleaves of *The*
Collected Poems Of Wallace Stevens

BUDDHA HEAD

For Nina Subin

Does it really matter that his body has disappeared?
His head, atilt on the pedestal of an open stone collar,
rests on banyan roots writhing like a fabulous beast body,
    as if this open collar were entrance to
an underworld where human souls sought out the souls of
elephants & snakes, & in that realm, where all
instruction comes from the other side of nature,
        "we" finally became a we
        rippling with imago mundi amplitude…

But what his obscure throat has led me to
is invisible, isn't it?   Visible,
this weather-stained limestone head, a parched field,
& five aerial roots dangling above his top-knot,
as if the vectors for a speech-balloon,
as if the banyan foliage were his thoughts…
    And if so, what might they be?

"At the point you rise from the soil, dear humans,
impact yourself with otherness, be twisted,
squeeze from your eyes the dog's tears, from your hearts
    the retch of the grasshopper's frozen violin…
but at the point you clear the veldt,
branch out, burgeon, attune yourselves to
the farthest point in space that you can imagine is also
    Jupiter for a bird,

& at the height of your own muscular observation,
go into the blue, dear humans,
triggered by the composted infinity all leave for all."

24 November, 1986

SMELLS CONFESSION

Creamed corn beef on toast for lunch 1949.
Mother's period. Her sad, love-needy eyes throughout the house.
Sparky's hair, pink-white dog skin, tight curly dog hair,
  & pups, just born, slimy, odor deeper than meat.
Fresh spring dirt in my first cave I dug in the backyard,
  they let me sleep in it. I put boards & a tarp on top.
My groin, say, at 10, on the toilet, faint semen odor.
Bath soap, new comic books; I'd smell the center, page by page,
versus newsprint, still woody. Versus shoulder-padding,
  sweated through, never dry through August football practice,
cotton molding with us, our pain & stupidity was it?
To let coach George Gale put us through tackling lines
  hitting held dummies 4 hours, 100 degrees Indianapolis heat
versus Caryl's sweet neck versus
seared Cajun steak versus
washer powered chemical sweet soap powder,
human versus dog excrement, one's own farts bizarrely
  smell ok,   what is it about our own shit *doesn't* stink?
mother's period, thin sweet tea-like blood aroma,
  the darkened Sunday house—
what am I remembering here?
                              My life as other-than-human,
whirlpool of the body, natural mind to recall & respect
  tender odor as real as paradise, or its outer edges,
the waft from the deep through which a terrier pants
  looking up, on her side, at me, another pup.

11 July 1995

A POEM & SOME NOTES ON AIMÉ CESAIRÉ

In 1978, I tried to explain to Florence Loeb, the daughter of the famous Parisian art dealer, the desire for the prodigious in Césaire's poetry & some of the circumstances under which it takes root. She listened to me, & then said something I will never forget: "Césaire uses words like the nouveaux riches spend their money." She meant, of course, that this prodigal son of France, educated & acculturated by France, should cease his showing off, racing his language like roman candles over her head, & return to the fold (to the sheepfold, I might add, to a disappearance among the millions for whom to have French culture is supposed to be more than enough). To this aristocratic woman, Aimé Césaire's imaginative wealth looked like tinsel. I carried this sinister cartoon of his power around with me for a couple of years. One morning what I wanted to say was a response to Césaire himself:

For Aimé Césaire

Spend language, then, as the nouveaux riches spend money
invest the air with breath newly gained each moment
hoard only in the poem, be the reader miser, a new kind of snake
coiled in the coin-flown beggar palm, be political, give it all away
one's merkin, be naked to the Africa of the image mine in which
biology is a tug-of-war with deboned language in a tug-of-war
    with
Auschwitz in a tug-of-war with the immense demand now to meet
    the complex
actual day across the face of which Idi Amin is raining—
the poem cannot wipe off the blood
but blood cannot wipe out the poem

CLAYTON ESHLEMAN

black caterpillar
in its mourning leaves, in cortege through the trunk of the high-
   way of
history in a hug-of-war with our inclusion in
the shrapnel-elite garden of Eden.

Re "nigger" Césaire told us to use the most offensive word in English
when translating the word. For the general public, "noir" and "negre"
may well have been interchangeable, but the very civilized & very
complexed Antilleans considered themselves as "Noirs," the "negres"
being on that distant continent, Africa. It is in this light that one must
read Césaire's use of the word "negre" & its derivatives "negritude,"
"negrillon" (nigger scum), & "negraille" (little nigger): he was mak-
ing up a family of words based on what he considered to be the most
insulting way to refer to a black.

What do I think of when I think of Césaire's poetry? Solemnity,
ferocity, tenderness & surprise, as well as his unique combination of
profound mythological confidence & linguistic botanical precision.

During one of our conversations, Césaire told me that he regarded
speech vagueness on the part of the colonized as one of the most de-
bilitating results of colonization. Later I found this pertinent quota-
tion from a 1960 interview:
   "I am an Antillean. I want a poetry that is concrete, very Antillean,
Martinican. I must name Martinican things, must call them by their
names. The cañafistula mentioned in "Spirals" is a tree; it is also
called the drumstick tree. It has large yellow leaves and its fruit are
those big purplish bluish black pods, used here also as a purgative.
The balisier resembles a plantain, but it has a red heart, a red flores-
cence at its center that is really shaped like a heart. The cecropias are

shaped like silvery hands, yes, like the interior of a black's hand. All of these astonishing words are absolutely necessary, they are never gratuitous…"

Like Artaud, Césaire positioned himself at the edge of Surrealism & assembled a poetic identity that was not limited to Surrealist aesthetics. Césaire might be said to have injected French Surrealism with a Martinican political consciousness, & an arcane & scientific vocabulary based not only on Martinican flora & fauna but African words as well. In Césaire's early poetry (up through *Solar Throat Slashed*), there is a shamanic enthusiasm for the marvelous & the ancient that evokes African animism.

2012

ARTICULATED HANDS

Hans Bellmer at Ubu Gallery, NYC, 17 March 2009

Spindle jointed fingers sewing
or rowing limb-wise,
limb-swept buttock skiffs in fugal matrimony—
finger pincered card-like decks,
gamble strewn swinging anagrams
swivel honed,
uroboros flexed.

Bone in bone   starts up
again,   didn't end,
did it ever begin? Or
are the sexes in infinite *media res*?
Geared see-saw intercourse,
bodies copulating as well with the bodies within,
which rise at night,
cobra hoods with message venom.

What do they wish to say?

"We are fused in semen
eggy seas opening as dream craters,
protozoic pillars
upon which imagination suns itself.
Vulva-breathing bubbles,
the Muse as a ball-jointed causation circuit
at blood tide with the mother Minotaur,
all bone & ooze,

socket of the sink hole ink flow.
Hoods which are the subjectiles
subjugating your scrimshaw."

MFA, Boston, "Titian, Tintoretto, Veronese" 21 March, 2009

Pope Paul III (Titian, 1543) Velvet tent-
                    esque cloak,
amber brown, over a skeletal body

   Fashionable hermits,
         child angels

   Strangle hold of the church
on Venetian imagination
     The bold chimpanzee of light
         & dark

The naked female body:
  the soft target of male mildew,
      or the god himself as
  a shower of urine-gold coins

   (soft fat flesh
   unsavory white,
     alabaster albino mud)

      Early filling-station:
        Venus, with Cupid-wrapped calf,
       squirting gas

    Tintoretto's contrasts:
      fulgurating light, bald & bushy dark

Winged babies—what to make of *them*?
Gutterflies? Baby flesh asail,
messengers of what Venus
            must face
        in her rear mirror?

        Saint Jerome entombed in
the shell of his pink cloak. Below him:
a dark-sniffing lion of Oz

No genitalia   swaddling-obscene

        Perseus in propellered sandals—
terrific vertical descent   over
        the monster's spiked cactus-pad
                wing
            veined ochre
            veined with alarm

    Late Titian,   saints shadow-gored
like stretch-marks or gouge lanes,
        the painter gripping the being-entombed-
Jesus's blood-tarred right breast

        Tintoretto's *Baptism of Christ* 1580
(he's 52)   light
        as solvent,   its drench-spiked
            anthem,
        John the Baptist
                    swinging out of

CLAYTON ESHLEMAN

prehistoric negritude
to tilt the bap-cup

& the sky! Mandalaed with gold!

Christ curtsies   as
the lyre pours out.

NOTES ON RHIZOMIC IDENTITIES / Focus of Week 3,
Naropa 2009

Gilles Deleuze and Felix Guattari: "A rhizome as subterranean stem
is absolutely different from roots and radicals. Bulbs and tubers are
rhizomes… Burrows are too, in all their functions of shelter, supply,
movement, evasion, and breakout. The rhizome itself assumes very
diverse forms, from ramified surface extension in all directions to
concretion into bulbs and tubers… The rhizome includes the best and
the worse; potato and couch grass or the weed… A rhizome cease-
lessly establishes connections between semiotic chains, organizations
of power, & circumstances relative to the arts, sciences, and social
struggles… A rhizome has no beginning or end; it is always in the
middle, between things, interbeing, *intermezzo*."

Pierre Joris: "What is needed now is a nomadic poetics. Its method
will be *rhizomatic:* which is different from collage i.e., a rhizomatics is
not an aesthetics of the fragment, which has dominated poetics since
the romantics even as transmogrified by modernism, high & low, &
more recently retooled in the neoclassical form of the citation—ironic
and/or decorative—throughout what is called "postmodernism."
Strawberry Fields Forever. A nomadic poetics will cross languages, not
just translate, but write in all or any of them. If Pound, Joyce, Stein,
Olson, & others have shown the way, it is essential now to push the
matter further, again, not so much as "collage" (though we will keep
those gains) but as a material flux of language matter. To try & think,
then, of this matter as even pre-language, proto-semantic, as starting
from what Julia Kristeva calls the *chora,* which she defines as "a tem-
porary articulation, essentially mobile, constituted of movements and
their ephemeral stases." And then to follow this flux of ruptures & ar-
ticulations, of rhythm, moving in & out of semantic & non-semantic

CLAYTON ESHLEMAN

spaces, moving around & through the features accreting as poem, a lingo-cubism, no, a lingo-barocco that is no longer an "explosante fixe" (Breton) but an "explosante mouvante."

Deleuze and Guattari: "The rhizome is an anti-hierarchical means of organizing knowledge and of recognizing intersections and engagements between seemingly disparate ideas & things. Botanically, the rhizome is a branching that has no 'center.' All segments are fertile. Any segment broken off from the rest may serve as a new starting point, a new origin of life. As a heterogeneous composition, it brings all manners of materials into productive contact with one another. In contrast to the tree: knowledge organized around & branching out of a central 'trunk.' In the arboreal system, 'trunk' is understood as the origin, source of authenticity or authority. Its branches are mere iterations or representations of their own content."

Clayton Eshleman: To think of the rhizome in the sense that Deleuze & Guatttari are describing takes me back to the origin of the metaphor at around 30,000 B.P.: juxtaposition of a vulva & horse head engraved in a limestone slab (the two equal in size, slightly overlapping, & incised with three cupules, one before the horse head, one as the horse's eye, & one in the center of the vulva). The metaphor and the meander (the basis for Aurignacian "art" which was rediscovered by Jackson Pollock in the American 1940s) seem to me to be the rootstock of imagination, or the fold between no image of the world & *an* image.

Joris: "Metaphor" may be a difficult one as it is easily a hierarchical, vertical situation, an attempt at transcendence. I wonder if in the case of the cave material & Pollock if 'image' isn't the better word. What Pollock produces is an image in process that is finished when the energy, physical and psychic, that he pours in, runs out ("a painting is never finished, it is abandoned"). In the cave work what is absolutely fascinating for me is the mass of drawings, one next to, over, or across another, with something of an implied equivalence between them. Not one of the cave drawings, not one of Pollock's squiggles or canvases is "it" i.e., THE metaphor for art, life, the godhead, the master-piece-that-says-it-all. Your "juxtaposition of a vulva & a horse head" doesn't necessarily seem to create a metaphor, but is a complex image, with no need to elevate them into what could only be some sort of abstract transcendental unity.

Eshleman: I feel that metaphor is neither vertical nor horizontal. How is "love is a red, red rose" hierarchical? It is an intensification, a sensualization of an otherwise abstract term—love—that is often involved in an idealistic, hierarchical system. The literal is hierarchical. The Bible read literally results in the saving of believers & the burning of non-believers, total lowering, total raising. I think of metaphor as fusion ("my eyes are fix'd / in happy copulation"), as a new creation, a third. God is an absolute, a one, not a metaphor. The shaman is a metaphor (as is "I," as Rimbaud astutely stated) because he is a fusion that participates in both the human & the animal realms.

Deleuze & Guattari we must keep in mind (I am thinking, having not read them, knowing them only via scattered quotations) are secondary thinkers whose work places them in the middle of something else. Aurignacian meander "systems" have many beginnings & many ends. It seems to me that primary thinkers involved in what we can call the autonomous imagination make use of arboreal metaphors as well as rhizomic ones; that is, a creative project determines its own vectors, designs, limitations, signatures as it moves out, or in. You also wrote that a truly open field has no up/down, front/back. But rhizomes themselves send out tendrils, or rootlets up, & below, as they themselves project horizontal movement. So they are somewhat tree-like in this regard.

Joris: I think the difference here is, to use Deleuze and Guattari again, that trees cannot transform their individual (hierarchical) parts (roots/trunk/branches) into each other (they are fixed, in that sense) while rhizomatic plants can & do all the time. But you are right in saying that major artists use both—though their tree or hierarchical structures are often what is or remains the least interesting (Dante is a great poet despite the Christian hierarchy that is structurally & in every other way the core to his poem; same goes for most of, though not all of, the religious art of the Renaissance—which we appreciate in spite of the doctrinal underpinnings).

Eshleman: Gerritt Lansing's early book is entitled *The Heavenly Tree Grows Downward*. How do you understand this? One approach would be to say that Lansing is interested more in the rootwork of a tree than in its foliage. Years ago, I thought he was plunging the tree into the earth & reversing its flow. But now I think that the direction he is interested in is underworld, root realm, & the nourishment of earth to root, versus branch to air. However, all this may be moot, as the tree in its full environment draws upon air & earth. The first World Tree is in Le Combel, a section of the Pech Merle cave: it is a stalagmitic formation with a vulvar fissure in its base & breast-like pod shapes above (daubed with black manganese by Cro-Magnons between 18,000 & 16,000 B.P.) This form is a Black Goddess too, as the "tree" is also a "woman." There is a photo of this amazing figure in *Juniper Fuse*, p. 211.

Joris: Gerritt comes out of a very hierarchical (the magical, hermetic, etc) tradition. One could see his tree as an attempt to exactly reverse this, to upset the apple-cart (while still keeping an inverted hierarchical order of the universe going). I think the poems are often better than what the title's indications/limitations propose.

Eshleman: Northrop Frye calls Blake's "The Marriage of Heaven & Hell" an anatomy, because it is made up of varying literary genres. This thought crossed my mind while I was working on "Notes on a Visit to Le Tuc d'Audoubert" & helped me understand the overall form of *Juniper Fuse* as a giant anatomy. It occurs to me that William Carlos Williams' *Paterson* (with his father/son hierarchical title) is a marvelous example of an *anatomy,* in a way that must be related to rhizomic theory. From *Paterson:*

> a mass of detail
> to interrelate on a new ground, difficultly;
> an assonance, a homologue
> > > triple piled
> pulling the disparate together to clarify
> and compress...

You write that one aspect of rhizomic theory as you understand it is a poetics that will cross languages. Lucky you with four. As a monolingual Hoosier I have tendril forays into Spanish and French but I cannot write in either.

Did Deleuze & Guattari consider Antonin Artaud to be a rhizomic writer? I wonder, since Artaud was so body-centered (the screaming body, ceaselessly attacked, in constant self-defense) that I see him as a kind of St. Sebastian nailed to the World Tree. His writings & drawings are replete with disconnects, detours, dead ends, sound syllables

& mythic grabs, but he has always seemed to me as one who fought to maintain a central core (for had he lost that, he would have been dispersed into insanity like the typical maniac).

***

NOTE: The Deleuze & Guattari quotation is from *A Thousand Plateaus,* University of Minnesota Press, 1987. The Joris quote is from his collection of essays, *A Nomadic Poetics,* Wesleyan University Press, 2003. Eshleman's *Juniper Fuse: Upper Paleolithic Imagination & the Construction of the Underworld* was also published by Wesleyan University Press in 2003.

The one captured Mombai terrorist
led into the mortuary & shown his 9 companions' remains
suddenly realized he had been duped.
Odd. Did he expect them not to be there? Or to be there
as a host of angels? Or, to have found the slabs bare,
the dead having ascended?

We know he knew all were to die, un-captured,
after they killed as many as they could.
What I would have given to have been in this young man's head
the moment he saw these ravaged remains. A Woody Allen moment,
when grandpa climbs out of his casket
& does a little dance before the assembled mourners.
Or a Boschian twinkling, St Anthony, surrounded by
a carnival of temptations hissing & hooting,
looks back, across centuries of the dead, at you & me,
two fingers raised. Like snail horns?
Who has been cuckolded? Not
the hissing & hooting temptations—
as Bosch's imagination
they are using Anthony as their dance floor.

2009

CLAYTON ESHLEMAN

The image is the place where I put on my soul
as if it were an inner lining, or a line
I can reach here, say, one I would drape around me
& then throw off, a death line
twisting down into those depths they say cannot be fathomed,
Cro-Magnon sensations, Neanderthal knots,
earliest shamanic accord, a cord then by which
a master spirit might climb, spinal,
electric with tantrik lesion, so do I sense my Muladhara Chakra
molt the serpent lounge latent in
that magic region Artaud so feared—between anus & sex,
the lower mid-point where the soul snake sleeps
—wonderful idea, all our lives? Through
everything?—until we whistle her up (I assume she)
& she rises along our spines, in the fantasy that sperm
   & brain
might wed, or are already wed, that the mind is a masculine
spermal animalcule, & that we are frequented
   by a feminine force…
I do not think my Muladhara is feminine
nor do I identify my imagination as masculine.
I reject duality of the spirit & vote for the orgy of
contested mind, lines in contest to
realize soul, the image in exile
beckoned by the bathyscope of the poem
lowered into places squirrels reflect, or robins
ruminate, animal lager… for the shaman from the start has
a bull's head, which means he spans
the I & other of formative consciousness.

Artaud feared the Muladhara because he believed God
would murder him there. Interesting. That God is most active
on the balance pan between shit & sperm
HE KILLS AT FULCRUM
anyone, especially one seeking to be fully born.
God certainly exists. He is at throne in man's Muladhara,
blood vessels like ranging choirs hallow him by the moment.
He is what we have deposited of
fruitless immortality into flesh & the legacy of flesh.
God exists as an escalator into nerve & muscle work,
as a human death-hate aggrandized into a celestial volcano hovering
love.

13 Dec 2010

A TANTRIK KEELSON

I sought to seal my destructiveness,
to ogle its principle feelers.
    Dionysus appeared,
        then Apollo, milled vertebrae,
    swarmed lancer. I attempted to mix my Africa
      with my Amazon.
Each anaconda presented a cove
pinked with feminine undertow,
fused & refused by masculine shimmy.

Sweetness through endless conflict,
sweetness at every point, even in pointillistic
    drops, the ocean that we are,
beyond outer space, proclaims.

I've worked for years to overstand the underglade,
to realize yin as positive, since I believe in
    a Tantrik keelson,
& have had an accordion experience with Caryl,
the two of us compressed & expanded,
in bellows to matter, inhabiting a dyadic groove.

All of the above is human, but psychological,
part of the paradise of the interior.
Since we are, when we are open, run through by
    human horror,
I also have to wonder about the lemur, & her
impression of night traffic outside the zoo.
I have to see my love & my Dionysus

in the context of a zoo,
Africa become zoo, Amazon. An anaconda begging
from pier to pier, the fabulous pink of male & female
    mixtures
on sale at The Gap. Across tilting planes,
occasionally, I talk with dead Nora Jaffe—
is this her or my stamina? How explain her instructions
    to me here? I am eager to peel
apples for her, more eager to cook for Caryl.
Divided, dyadic, afraid that I may reDarger as a caterpillar
or enghost as a Chinese bride
wearing an extraordinary menstrual hut.
Something in me shouts at me:
eat the gore of Iraq!
Which, if I could do so my body tells me,
appetite & the world would coadunate.
Time
to imaginalize everything.

2003–2017

AXIS RESOURCE

I have had to create my own ancestors.
I dumped the Eshlemans decades ago, never met the Spencers.
Intuiting that it was impossible to ignite sacred fire off oneself,
I went to Powell,
   Vallejo, Coatlicue, Yorunomado.
These eidola I placed around me, a cromlech of mouth stones,
   Orphic beheadeds—

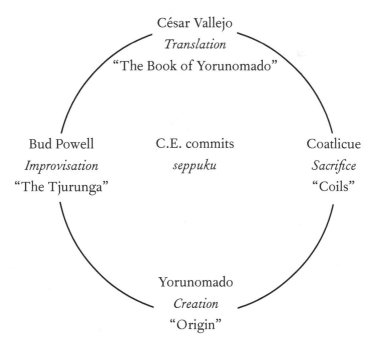

Once the self is constellated, meaning comes with it.

The fullness of life—as set against the void—how to measure it?

During a spring 1963 Kyoto party, Gary Snyder dancing with the host
    while throwing
the guy's shoji screens out into the creek behind the house.

I'd also like to honor Antonin Artaud strolling Blvd Montparnasse,
    1947, his arm
around 16 year old Florence Loeb, offering her avuncular advice
    about virginity!

Or the expression on Aimé Césaire's face as he scurried across a traf-
ficked street near the Sorbonne, 1978, while accompanying me to a
café where he would respond to my list of translator questions.

        Such moments are so rich, so close to
    a dear kiss,   life swells,   percolates…

                                        4 December 2010

SWEETHEART

For Caryl Eshleman's 60th Birthday

Putting MSM cream on your back,
watching the white work into the gold,
shoulder blades, latissimus, the top of each shoulder,
wondering how this substance brings relief.

You stand naked on the bathroom mat,
grateful for an hour of minimal pain.

Feeling your flesh & bone work:
can fantasy & biography mesh?

It has been 19 years since I wrote:
"You are oysters cigarettes a radio"
—third line of a 40 line poem I couldn't finish,
each line for a year of your life.

Today I'd like to display your sweetness in strata,
bed upon bed, chrysalis & imago.

    *

You are a bawling caterpillar, a puppy snarled in her own wings.

So tasty the incubus harpies have already spotted you from their heli-
    copter eyries.

In the 1946 VJ Night neighborhood celebration, a 4 year old out
    alone, tasting beer, miraculously steered home/

At 7, you told 9-year-old Susan Brotsky, & her mother that you knew
   what a period was. Amazed, they said, "well, what is it?" "The dot
   at the end of a sentence."

By constellating & naming stars humans have tried to make them
   their own—but is there a mouse constellation? A constellation for
   your dog you named Chubby?

With hair set by your mother with water & sugar, what sweetness the
   bees tasted intoxicated by the little blonde lost in high grass a few
   years from home.

Caryl Reiter with a dog-collar ankle bracelet. Caryl Reiter with sling-
   back black shoes.

Caryl Reiter grown beyond pinafores in a stretchtop with a topless
   brassiere, nylons on Sunday because her Catholic friend wore
   them, in leopard pants, lipstick painted over her lips

You stopped & talked with the poor soul masturbating under the
   Coney Island boardwalk.

Raped, you refused your friend's offer to break the Greek's legs.

You dreamed you were a stone lady holding up a building. The only
   thing alive was your cunt, was there for lonely men, just to fuck
   them—if they knew enough to fuck you then they knew your cunt
   was alive.

We rented a Volkswagen one Sunday, spring 1970, drove to Harriman
   State Park & ate acid in the woods. Filled with that poison I began

CLAYTON ESHLEMAN

to shout for Hollie, my "new" Marie, another person I had chosen to desire as self-torture. We came back to the car at dusk. You had your camera—we started taking pictures of each other over the back of the Volkswagen. Once, looking through the lens I saw you—Caryl—not La Muerte, femme fatal, or housewife, but an exasperated, sweating woman who was original! Not the image of Woman, not superficial; fresh.

When you were married in your late teens to Alan, you told your mother you were taking ergot to abort. "It's not going to work," she said. "Why?" "Because I took it before I had you.

From time to time, as if from a dry basin of stillness, I hear you say: "I have nothing to do." Is that ergot moment the burn spot in your peacock ledger?

The chunks of jasper we collected in Utah—I keep 3 on my desk under the bookshelf where the image of Faye Dunaway is assimilated into your specific loveliness.

Thoughts of you conjure the *granit rose* of Tregastel, undulant Daliesque near-forms tawny in mid-morning sunlight, or the dove-grey, ochre limestone cliffs wandered by long black stains as we approach Les Eyzies on D47 from Périgueux.

Lespinasse, 1974: we carried our dinner outside to the stone table on the landing by the door to our second floor Bouyssou apartment. The farm was on a rise which sloped down through an apple orchard. When we sat down to eat, well before sunset, we had for entertainment an extraordinary sky. Clouds would come floating over the woods, spreading out over us. Puff collisions, Mickey Mouse ears, shredding gargoyles, turrets, vales, mammoth apparitions densifying & disintegrating as they appeared. Many reminded us of the images we were trying to make out on the cave walls. To sit at that stone table—what an experience—to be in love there, at one of the most vital times in our many years together. Much of what happened—the "event aspects"—during our first spring & summer in the Dordogne is now as dispersed as the clouds we used to watch—yet it billows in us, an inclusive cloud whose heart is ours.

Getting up in the middle of the night at the farm you spotted a large lavender spider in the middle of the kitchen floor. You let out your spider scream, & the spider, making tapping noises on the linoleum, ran under the stove. The next morning, after trapping the spider in a shoe box & removing it from our apartment, I ate a small alive spider to calm you.

"How do you feel about your body?" the LA physical therapist, after asking you to take off all but your panties, inquired. Your response as you stood before him was, for me, Aphrodite ascending.

Going over worksheet after worksheet with me, at the table in the morning after coffee, asking me thousands of questions: what did I mean by this, why did I write that, helping me to narrow down the infernal discrepancy between what I thought I had written & what I did write. While I went into the labyrinth on my own & sometimes emerged, at the center you were the companion providing resistance, neither Minotaur nor Falconress.

Devonshire, 1979: your utter accessibility, your head tilted under green apples, your sweetness sweetness, your tart light heart-sown, your hair blown sweetness.

I love to watch you eat fresh Dungeness crab—your plate heaped
with cracked ice, topped by a reconstruction of the crab. Over
which your delicate fingers—more delicate than the morsels you
will extract—pause like wands, & you slowly eat, as if you were
undoing a sewing, as if your fingers are needles investigating
music, or thinking about "The most sublime act is to set another
before you," which can refer to any act of respect for the otherness
all nearness is, not to be worshipped but revered in motion, in
pleasure scythed & harvested, a beautiful creature eating a beauti-
ful creature.

You've made a half-dozen photo collages with us, friends, & places.
In the downstairs bathroom today I stopped before you in your
Italian blue jump suit with flared legs & sleeves (in which you
danced upstairs at Max's Kansas City). On another wall there's a
photo of you smiling in the raccoon jacket I bought you on St.
Mark's Place—you're wearing it with my crushed-velvet rust
pants, wide leather belt & scarlet sweater. The fur turns henna in
the 1969 autumn sunlight.

I look for words for what being inside you is, the thought makes me
shake, empty quivers like Songs of Songs volley about. To place
myself inside you & not hurt you, to be at the heart of your life, to
slightly know you where only you know yourself, to have this
billygoat extension encased, a warm oar as if in the first the very
first waters.

After dinner, 1982, in a Paris bistro otherwise forgotten, a dog jumped
up next to you on the banquette, sat there looking up politely, a
pug, big ET eyes, smashed truffle nose. Just sat there, happy. So I
went out to the kitchen & asked about the dog. The chef said: "He

stays with me in the kitchen until I finish cooking, then goes out
into the restaurant & chooses someone to sit by. He's Belgian, a
Brabancon. The males are good-natured—the females are very
bitchy. They have small bottoms & have to deliver a big head."

Your assemblage in the dining room corner: on an old ironing board a
wood skateboard holding up your sculpture of my head in unfired
clay, flanked by a stuffed rabbit lady & a photo of a white gorilla.
Beyond each end of the skateboard, a *tanuki* with ground-length
balls, sake jug, & chin-tied straw hat—& a pot-bellied Balinese
wood frog with a leaf parasol. Scattered about on the ironing
board: a clay Oaxacan lady holding a duck & a squash with a cut
watermelon on her head by Joséfina Aquilar, many little pigs
(falling on their backs, doing head stands), a 19th century iron that
used coal, a rabbit with a carrot candle stick, & a salt & pepper set
of two little fat rabbits. It is our *ofrenda*.

Your gold ring which you designed & cast, with its undulant creased
leaf base mounted with a rosette enchased with a garnet & a half-
moon of 7 tiny diamonds across the diamondless third of the
rosette, a furrowed sweep of gold, carotene river as close to me as
the Styx.

[1981–2001]

A NOTE ON BUD POWELL & IMPROVISATION

I started glancing at *Downbeat* magazine, around 1951, when I was sixteen years old & a student at Shortridge High School in Indianapolis, Indiana. While I had been taking piano lessons initially from a neighborhood piano teacher & later from the concert pianist Ozan Marsh, I was only vaguely aware of the existence of jazz. I taped two quarters to a *Downbeat* order form & mailed it off for a 45 RPM recording with Lennie Tristano's "I Surrender, Dear" on one side, & Bud Powell's "Tea for Two" on the other.

The simple armature of that tune engulfed in improvisational glory roared through my Presbyterian stasis, sinking a depth charge into my soul-to-be. I listened to it again & again, trying to grasp the difference between the lyric & what Powell was doing to it. Somehow an idea vaguely made its way through: you don't have to play someone else's melody—you can improvise, make up your own tune! WOW—really? You mean, I don't have to be my parents? I don't have to "play their melody" for the rest of my life?

The alternative—being myself—was a stupendous enigma that took me another six years to begin to approach. I had to get completely bored with all the possibilities my given life had prepared me for (including playing the piano) before I could make a grab at something that challenged me to change my life.

Later I realized that Powell had taken the trivial in music (as Art Tatum did with "I'll See You in My Dreams") and transformed it into an imaginative structure. William Carlos Williams, I noted, had done something similar in poetry. Alan Groves has written: "From 1947 to 1953 Powell was the supreme jazz pianist. These mature years produced some of the most startling piano ever recorded. Most of the best of his high-speed linear improvisations build toward a continuous driving climax. His lines would be based on a tune's chordal structure but flowed independently of it."

While reading the Sunday newspaper Comics on the living-room floor was probably my first encounter, as a boy, with imagination, Powell was my first encounter, as an adolescent, with the force of artistic presence, & certainly the key figure involved in my becoming a poet.

In my book *The Gull Wall* (1975) I wrote a poem which brooded about Powell's tragic life & about what he had offered me in 1951 which, in the writing of the poem, cut all the way back to the neighborhood piano teacher lessons my mother started me on when I was 6:

> Bud Powell
> locked in his Paris bathroom so he wouldn't wander.
> Sipping his lunch from the cat
> saucer on the floor.
> I see him curled there, nursing his litter,
> his great swollen dugs,
> his sleepy Buddha face
> looks down through the lotus pond,
> sees the damned, astral miles below,
> amongst them a little unmoving Clayton Jr.,
> placed by his mother on a bed of keys.
> Powell compassionately extended his tongue,
> licked my laid out senses.

Concerning the imagery in this poem: in 1954, Altevia Edwards, nicknamed Buttercup, became Powell's common-law wife & manager. She & Powell lived in Paris from 1959 to 1962, during which time Bud's alcoholism nearly killed him. During this period, Buttercup

CLAYTON ESHLEMAN

collected his earnings, held his passport & papers, & denied him any real degree of independence. I read somewhere that when Buttercup would leave her & Powell's hotel room she would lock him into the bathroom & deposit what she thought of as his lunch in a dish on the floor. This story was the source of some of the imagery in the poem just quoted, which also included my improvisation on what I under-stood to be Powell's pathetic situation as well as his extraordinary gift to me.

In bebop, musical structures & performance events shift between fixed or unfixed aspects, sometimes occupying both simultaneously. For a pianist like Powell, rapid melodic lines in the right hand would be punctuated by irregularly spaced, dissonant chords in the left. Fixed aspects would include pre-existing harmonic sources, such as the chord progressions in "I Got Rhythm" whose original harmony became the basis for Powell's "Bud's Bubble," his new improvised "melody", so to speak. Other examples of well-known original har-monies & new, improvised melodies are "Cherokee" as the basis for "Koko," and "How High the Moon" for "Ornithology."

> Rounding the gym track listening to WEMU.
> Suddenly Sonny Stitt entangles "Koko" with my mental vines.

> "Cherokee" lyrics, schlock "Indian romance,"
> pulled inside out by "Koko," "Cherokee's" vital ghost.

In the mid-1980s I wrote a sestina fantasia based on Powell's eleven month hospitalization in 1947 in the Creedmore State Hospital where he was administered two series of electroshocks. It is said that he drew a keyboard on the wall of his cell so that he could mentally keep up his chops while incarcerated. In my poem I used material from the Odyssey as my "original harmony," & envisioned Powell as a kind of

Tiresias in the Odyssey's Book Eleven as my "new melody". Since a concert grand with raised lid resembles (from the position of the audience seated before it) a headless bison, I had Powell in the poem attempting to imbibe blood-like sustenance from his sketched "bison keyboard."

THE BISON KEYBOARD

Onto the keyboard of a concert grand Bud Powell shot his fingers

Was he, elbows flexed, a kind of Tiresias drinking from a trench
    beheaded bison blood?
Are we not, at birth, like bison, deposited on a terrestrial
    keyboard?
Each depressed key makes an omen trench.
Thus does the earth become grand
& we suck, with Tiresias intensity, as did infant Powell, to
    prophesy.

Powell is face to face with a bison apparition, a lacquered black
    ghost.
Unlike Tiresias, he must draw, through a keyboard, directional
    sound,
& even if he has a grand it is hardly a trench of warm blood.
To be a seer is to re-enter the trench out of which we emerged.
Powell made contact, but failed to drink.
For a grand, in profile, lid propped, evokes a headless bison,
whose chest cavity, the keyboard, releases sound Tiresias needed
    blood to utter.
And Tiresias, who re-entered the essential trench, did guide
    Odysseus.

CLAYTON ESHLEMAN

At the keyboard, Powell clawed for blood, as if stabbing at a bison
  sacrifice.
Thus he proposes a grand dilemma: the living, no matter how
  grand their C chords,
lack the Tiresian recipe: to be all soul & bison vivid, a
  cunnilinctrice of the goddess trench.

On his cell wall in Creedmore asylum, Powell is said to have
  sketched, in chalk, a keyboard.

Powell, now the ghost of a grand, stared at this keyboard.
"O how get home, Tiresias? How drink bison music in this hellish
  trench?"

1/6/2016

Facing Pollock's "Number 1. 1949" at the Los Angeles Museum of
    Contemporary Art, 23 March, 2008 (First Take)

Work from the four sides
Method of Indian sand painters of the West

Crushed labyrinth
World map compressed into a folding abyss
Whirl dribble cream over depth's raised seams
tadpole verbs   the flit the loop of mind improvising
"Viento entero"   "Wind from All Compass Points"
blobs as nodes in liquefying constellations
Knot slipped warp   Cut woof   goose the nematodes
Blind mandrill in curlers & panties
Increase this pour to replicate being

—not my being but being's being as burgeoned through me

The head as a wedge to widen Eden, to strip it of cherub
Dip & swivel: masses of winter branches
    misted by the memory of elms
Composite face of leaves   face of Rothko's shotgun   face of knee
    mold
The century gushes in   Rein in, ride out the loyalty of painting
    snailing out of tailspin
Orchid ugly mauve blocked circumstance
Cro-Magnon shadows: riot of the stone wall in those who seek
    an easel explanation
Ape with bright orange buttocks: explode your monotheistic throne

Plumb the cracks   Enweb the fissures
divine meaning in the marks the trail signs
Rorschach of this brail as you emptied turns into it
The it you mythomania   Watching the daggers prance
  on the dome of The Lord's Prayer

Volcano writing   Crawling beggar scrapes
What a million chickens have left on the floor
  that is a door into a million gummed eyes
Mumonkan sepulcher
Minotaur Theseus Ariadne
as fructifying germs buzzing a darkened shaft
whose apogee is swarmed by electric white.

HYBRID HIEROPHANIES

A very ancient image of the soul is seated, resting,
inside of a bison-headed man.
Apparently a young woman, she has an adolescent body,
her face is composed of slanted hair lines,
long head hair streams out of the hybrid's hump.
Her thin forearms slope forward to merge with his penis.

These two figures share three legs, two knees lifted,
as if dancing behind the inflated anus of a reindeer which
swerves its aurochs head to gaze at this anima in her "crib."
At Les Trois Frères, around 14,000 years ago,
the hybrid is the engine of anima display.

To hybridize is to improvise. The hybrid is not only the engine of
    anima display
but the creator of imagination in folklore & the historic arts.

The word "hybrid" comes from the Latin *hybrida,* defined as "the
piglet resulting from the union of wild boar with tame sow." The
hybrida root stresses that the incongruity of the fusion derives not
from different species but from the intermingling of wild & tame
states. Translating these states into anthropological terms, it defines
aspects of both shamans & witches whose identities & activities are

    CLAYTON ESHLEMAN

comprised of wild & tame, or wilderness & cultural, experience. Concerning witches, Hans Peter Duerr writes:

"As late as the Middle Ages, the witch was still the *hagaꝫussa,* a being that sat on the *Hag,* the fence which passed behind the gardens and separated the village from the wilderness. She was a being who participated in both worlds. As we might say today, she was semi-demonic. In time, however, she lost her double features and evolved more and more into a representative of what was being expelled from culture, only to return, distorted, in the night."

This *hagaꝫussa,* "the one riding the fence," may be indirectly connected to, or correspond to, the bird-headed man in Lascaux's Shaft who appears to be reaching for, or dropping, a bird-headed staff. As part of his ritual paraphernalia, this staff, or "conductor baton," synchronizes with the fence on which the witch symbolically "rides," her magical animal before it acquired the meaning of "rod." The phallus is implicitly part of this scene, & human coitus with an animal is evoked. Initially, then, male & female shamans may have been the *hybrida* of wild animal & tame human marriages.

##

The hybrid image resonates throughout the Upper Paleolithic with a stylistic range that includes unidentifiable fragmentary figures. These may have been scratched on cave walls in the dark along with extremely sophisticated fusions that attest to a much more thorough transformation than men wearing masks. Such hybrids indicate not only a proto-shamanism but other goals similar to those of countless historical shamanic quests: the recovery of that first unbroken condition when the thoughts & desires of men & women were in fluid & absolute accord with the terrestrial & animal energies surrounding them.

The self,
a hybridizing amoeba jerking to
its wounds,
peering forth from its mammoth
cradle as if
off the planet's edge.

What a drop
25,000 years compose!
What a Fall
from man exterior to mammoth
to man lodged
mutilated in
a hybrid head.

I am staggered by the effort that was needed on the part of Cro-Magnon people to transform sexual/survival energies. Out of a world that strikes me as being, at the same time, ferocious, subtle, omen-perforated, magical and very utilitarian—or out of a void in which all these forces intermingled, there were people capable of inventing themselves, along with what appears to be much of what we hold to be human today. What was behind this thrust into imagination? I envision a crisis that slowly came to a head over thousands of years in which hominid animality eroded, & at around 35.000 B.P. began to be separated out of to-be-human heads, & daubed, smeared, & chipped onto cave walls lit solely by hand lamps.

On a conical rock pedant near the end of the End Chamber in Chauvet, arching over the legs & vulvic triangle of a "Venus" figure is a detailed bison head with chest & hump. For a front leg the bison has a thin human arm with long fingers extending into the "Venus's" left leg. It appears that these two figures have been drawn on a feline's head & upper body positioned on the curving side of the rock pedant. The accelerator mass spectrometry date for these figures is 30,340 B.P. Not only do they appear to be the earliest augur of the "Minotaur" & "Venus" figures; they are also the earliest indication of a hybrid proto-shamanic male figure in a protective or even "reverential" position over a woman.

Bison are the most transmutable Upper Paleolithic animals. They appear in both male & female roles. Their heads & horns are usually associated with men, while their bodies sometimes relate to women. They appear to be the primary shamanistic animal "vehicle" until their disappearance due to the spread of forests. A few examples suggest their rich image range:

Male: the bison-headed men in Les Trois Frères & possibly the last hybrid in Gabillou; in Font-de-Gaume several of the bison heads in profile look like bearded men; the bison-horned figure with snarling mouth in La Pasiega; the Minotaur-like figure in Chauvet whose bent-over, curling body bears some resemblance to the bison-human hybrid carved in a stalagmite in El Castillo.

Female: the notched bison horn held up by the Venus of Laussel; the phallic bison standing over a supplicating pregnant woman on an engraved reindeer bone from Laugerie Haute; the possibly birth-giving bison at Altamira; the "bison-women" in Pech-Merle whose schematic hybrid bodies may be variations on the Aurignacian female profiles traced on the cave's ceiling; the third "Venus" at Angles-sur-l'Anglin who obliterates one bison & whose lower body is crossed by another bison; the reindeer-bison at Les Trois Frères, given the context, appears to be female, as does the disemboweled bison in the Lascaux Shaft.

Male/Female: in Le Tuc d'Audoubert a male bison (with convex eyes) may be mounting a female (with concave eyes); the two headless, embracing bison that are part of a spear-thrower found in Enléne.

1974: Gorge d'Enfer, across from the Les Eyzies train tracks & river, is a small valley where animals, some of which are descendants of those depicted by Cro-Magnon people, wander in semi-liberty. Caryl & I recall the utter strangeness of coming upon a small bison in a pen there. It stood motionless, in profile to us—in the same position that its ancestors were often drawn on cave walls. It seemed both less & more real than the paintings in nearby Font-de-Gaume, which, as we watched, seemed to hover between us & the living bison as if we were all figures in a dream in which bison & human beings, humped & hooded semblances, intersect through fog & blowing snow.

Henri Frankfort: "The Egyptian interpreted the nonhuman as super-human, in particular when he saw it in animals—in their inarticulate wisdom, their certainty, their unhesitating achievement, and above all in their static reality. With animals the continual succession of genera-tions brought no change. They would appear to share the fundamen-tal nature of creation." James Hillman continues these thoughts: "Each animal confirms that living forms continue, they are eternal forms walking around. An animal is eternity alive and displayed. Each giraffe and polar bear is both an individual here and now and the species itself, unchanging, always self-creating according to kind. Each polar bear presents the eternal return of the polar-bear spirit as a guardian, a *spiritus rector,* from which, according to Ivar Paulson speaking of the circumpolar arctic peoples, the very idea of a God arises. "Gods originated within the animal world itself, that is, within the actual animal."

The eagle of inspiration sinks talons into our shoulders,
lifting us up & off in flights to an underworld
echoing the Upper Paleolithic as well as 19th century North Ameri-
    can Plains.
        What are the ingredients of inspiration?
Spires of incest over the ages? Wirings short-circuited, then re-fused?
You is part pedestal, part sty, part abyss, part snake.
When I tunneled did the mud around me contain a cast of cells, cham-
    bers, cloisters,
every person with whom I have traded eyes,
nebula particles, all colors, inner space?
Rank ocelot aprowl in legends which enter me through the godspell
    of *you.*
The muse as *you,* Pandora's hexagrams bollixed with changes.

Palmed stone, horn fragment, oneself at womb when preconscious-
    ness
percolated as mother sub-consciousness through the caul.
You with its angel-insectile feelers rising like a jellyfish drawn up
through surging salt water by solar warmth.

##

The essence of human power:
access to the cosmos from the heavens down to
    earth & into Xibalba.
I have the tail of a snake, my head is wrapped in smoke scrolls.
I am the power behind conjuring, & let me tell you right off
how thin the smoky veil is
separating the supernatural from the natural.
There are shells attached to my body,

                              enema
is faster than oral ingestion,
                         I vomit
a decapitated head onto my jaguar kilt,
                                   I am Och Chan,
the bearded dragon,   macerated in a luxury of forces,
god flowers surface in my skin, I am
opossum in the darkest hours before daybreak,
the forehead torch from which waterlilies & seedpods erupt.
& Looking through the telescope of night, through its vehicular
    cinders,
I visited Charles Olson at his Matterhorn of apocatastasis.
He kissed my lunar eclipses, my burned, emergent, blood-let sylphs.

Xibalba, the dance floor under North America, the range,
forever vital in caricaturing us, shuffling our vows.

Give me your claw bundle, Walt Whitman,
your Maya hypodermics. Let me feel the efflux of soul
as these gods & lords milked you into existence.
High on coffee enema, have you a Thimble Theatre skit for us this
     evening?
Or are you now totally otherworldly,
a Xibalba denizen, decapitating any young poet whose neck is not
loadstone geared to dance your blade?

I keep having this fuzzy vision of a brain termite queen
pumping out image babies as other creatures blow into it.
Sirens, the nightside or ancient form of the Muse,
are said to suck the breath of the sick
& are associated with siesta nightmares.
"Muse" akin to *musus*, "animal muzzle,"
a Muse-muzzled succubus crawling across the dreamer
or up through the dreaming,
blowing the dreamer's mind,
mind ejaculating into Muse muzzle.

Eye holes of a crocodile mask:
portals into the moonlit gore of the animalistic soul.

The hell that is man mesmerizes the mind, as if to keep mind mantised
    on grief & torture,
when like solar sharks we should be cruising the Sombrero Galaxy...

Finnegan's Wake   "end again's wake"
Ah,   when did the end first wake?
When the stag-headed "Dancing Sorcerer," presiding several meters
    over
the tangled mass of animals engraved on the walls of Les Trois Frères,
    was first conceived?

Great full bosomed night, shower me with your Eleusinian brew,
your solar pyres & yes, Artaud screaming through the flames,
fill me with ergot ignition, I am levitant at the edge, self-propelled to
    imagine.
Let *Dinofelis* sniff what I perspire, get me close to the crucify crossway,
let me envision, night, your tiara & your sty.

The Cro-Magnon sensation of palpitating one's animal slant: no more.
Poussin's satyr-scape: no more.
The anointing of the dead Adonis: no more.
Pan's shadow in leafy quilts: no more.
Blind Orion searching for the risen sun: no more...
Charred girders call out to us. Screens of a stirring. Afterlife of the gone.

James Hillman: "This feeling of being loved by the images permeates
the analytical relationship. Let us call it *imaginal love,* a love based
wholly on relationship with images and through images, a love show-

ing in the imaginative response of the partners to the imagination in dreams. Is this Platonic love? It is like the love of an old man, the usual personal content of love voided by coming death, yet still intense, playful, and tenderly, carefully close."

As a pupa in the chrysalis of day, it has taken me a lifetime to gauge the congeries in the arc of night.

In Gargas, a Cro-Magnon placed his or her hand on the cave's wall,
spat red ochre around the hand, withdrew it,
leaving what we might call an I-negative on the wall...

Is what we now call art the sempiternal challenge of this I-negative—
Kafka's "What is laid upon us to accomplish is the negative,
the positive being already given?"

When I was six, my mother placed my hands on the keys.
At sixteen, I watched Bud Powell sweep my keys into a small pile,
then ignite them with his "Tea For Two."
The dumb little armature of that tune
engulfed in improvisational glory
roared through my Presbyterian stasis.
    "Wail"
    "Un Poco Loco"
sank a depth charge into
    my soul-to-be.

In bebop, musical structures and performance events shift between fixed or unfixed aspects, sometimes occupying both simultaneously. Rapid melodic lines in the right hand punctuated by irregularly spaced, dissonant chords in the left. Bud Powell's comping added to the bebop ensemble another layer of polyrhythms. The quality of his solos, their asymmetrical improvisations, long melodic lines that often overrode standard cadential resting points, extended the melodic, harmonic & percussive possibilities of the piano.

Dizzy Gillespie recognized the relationship between the spoken rhetoric of the hipster & the musical rhetoric of bebop: "As we play with musical notes, bending them into new and different meanings that constantly change, he plays with words."

The harmonic structure of "I Got Rhythm" won a place in Charlies Parker's imagination, much as the theme of the *Eroica* Variations or perhaps Diabelli's *Waltz* had in Beethoven's—though Beethoven concentrated his efforts on lengthy, integrated compositions, while Parker's "I Got Rhythm" variations are scattered widely among many performances.

Rounding the gym track, listening to WEMU.
Suddenly Sonny Stitt entangles "Koko" with my mental vines.
"Cherokee" lyrics, schlock "Indian romance,"
pulled inside out by "Koko," "Cherokee's" vital ghost.
    Euphoric zone where there's stride foam I can drink.
    Is it mitotic? Is it mine?

Theseus, a tiny male spider, enters a tri-level construction:
look down through the poem, you can see the labyrinth.
Look down through the labyrinth, you can see the spider-centered
    web.

                                  Coatlicue
      Sub-incision   Bud Powell
               César Vallejo
                    The bird-headed shaman

These nouns are also nodes in a constellation called
Clayton's Tjurunga. The struts are threads
in a web. There is life blood flowing through
these threads. Coatlicue flows into Bud Powell,
César Vallejo into sub-incision.

          The bird-headed shaman
is slanted under a disemboweled bison.
His erection tells me he is in flight. He drops
his bird-headed stick as he penetrates
    bison paradise.

The red sandstone hand lamp
abandoned below this scene
is engraved with vulvate chevrons—did it once flame
    from a primal sub-incision?

This is the oldest part of this tjurunga, its grip.

Hybrid figures are antennae reaching out from earthly matter: recipients of invisible forces. They partake of the nature of the shaman, & have become the satyrs & fauns of the Dionysian cult as well as the devils & imps of Christian art. Masks & hybrid creatures have this in common: it is impossible to grasp their meaning without bringing in the essential factor of indetermination between the real & the imaginary which constitutes their rightful being & nature.

In Donald Cordry's book *Mexican Masks* (1980), based on the author's some forty years of ethnographic research in many regions of Mexico, the finest featured mask maker is a mysterious figure named José Rodríguez who, according to Cordry, lived & worked as a goat-herder in one of the most remote mountain regions of the state of Guerrero. Rodríguez's art only became known to Cordry in 1975 when twenty-five of his masks were discovered in a village commissariat where they had hung for years. All of these masks which are carved from a single piece of hardwood supposedly had been used in rain-petitioning dances. In the way that they made use of various creatures they demonstrated Rodríguez's extraordinary skill & knowledge of Nahua symbolism. Cordry never met Rodríguez & gives the reader the impression that this master mask maker died long before his work came to the author's attention.

Cordry himself died in 1978. By the mid-1980s, it had become clear to a number of Mexican folk art specialists that Rodríguez was an utterly shadowy figure who might have never made masks or even existed. A few of these specialists have written that they have met a couple of the actual carvers & painters of the still so-called "Rodríguez masks." As for the stature of such masks, the specialists have dismissed them as decorative & inauthentic, meaning they were made to sell in markets & to collectors & never used in dances or other native ceremonies. In my opinion, these masks are extraordinarily powerful works of art & should be acknowledged as such & not savaged by a bogus "authentic" "decorative" duality.

In these masks the hybrid transmogrifies into a Mexican grotesque realism. The human face is transfixed in tumultuous, writhing halos of actual & imagined creatures, a kind of animal comeuppance as it were, as if the fauna world is in the process of exploring the Mexican soul in frenzies of adoration & bile, improvising a Medusaean pandemonium of exaltation & creature drapery.

In one mask a black-speckled snake coils down through a forehead, the snake's head becoming the face's nose between traumatized staring-down eyes, while lizards slither down both sides of the face, their eyes meeting where a throat might have been.

In another mask, a darkly-painted humanoid face has wide-open, circular spellbound eyes, an open puckering mouth with broken, fierce fangs, while foot-long black-spotted snakes pirouette on his skull. Below the chin is a crouching coyote-like creature framed by lizards posed on projecting branches.

Still another mask presents a swarthy human devil, tongue hanging out, his skull surmounted by a pink imp bracing flexed legs on top of two yellow frogs. The imp is gripping black & green mottled snakes which are wiggling down along each side of the devil's forehead.

Two frog-devil masks have crouching, frightened snake-crawled frogs with shocked open-mouthed human faces filling their backs.

A "corn-spirit" mask has a long-haired bearded male face topped by a sinister bat whose chest is crossed by two lizards that form its breasts. Serpents rise above the bat's head in the shape of open-mouth fanged corn-stalks. At the base of the mask, large cartoonish snake heads bare their fangs. Cordry comments that the characteristics of this mask suggest it is a version of The Lord of the Animals.

Such hybridity presents animal otherness as nightmarish projection & capture, as if the human head is an abyss populated by flurries of prancing, leering, and soul-pocketing guardians.

Firefly passes through jaguar
& jaguar tills the animal fields.
We walk the crocodile of the earth
& notice her birth hole,
out of which deer are streaming.
Spider is our black transformer,
her nets are gilded with rabbits & peccaries.
By stingray we are pressed to owl,
by owl we are intact in ceiba.
This is the living core of the world,
a vision of living shadows,
a vision of Itzamna's mind.

In Les Trois Frères, some fifty animals, mainly bison, in shapes from different periods, swarm the hopping bison-headed man with a female figure inside him. Most of the animals show signs on their bodies: V-shaped projectiles, barbed & parallel lines. A melee, animals intersecting animals, some in stampede, others in stasis. The churning turmoil is so intense that what meets the eye could be described as Upper Paleolithic Abstract Expressionism. The organic hybridity throughout the heads & bodies of these figures makes them truly fantastic & not merely human beings wearing ritual paraphernalia. Such thorough hybridity emphasizes their mental reality as figures that were imagined, dreamed or seen in trance.

CLAYTON ESHLEMAN

The 35,000-24,000 B.P. Aurignacian is the period in which the first image-making we now know of (in contrast to abstract marks, cupules, grids etc) took place. The kind of images vary considerably from region to region (crude engravings & meandering lines in the Dordogne & Arige; Chauvet's polychromatic splendor in the Ardéche). Not only is it time to let the Aurignacians have the floor but to acknowledge that they are the floor.

Jackson Pollock: "My painting does not come from the easel. I hardly ever stretch my canvas before painting. I prefer to tack the un-stretched canvas to the hard wall or the floor. I need the resistance of a hard surface. On the floor I am more at ease. I feel nearer, more a part of the painting, since this way I can walk around it, work from the four sides and literally be in the painting. This is akin to the method of the Indian sand painters of the West."

"To dissemble thus deny any fulcrum in this annexed
dark. An ark? Din of anodyne shadow passengers
entering. An Aurignacian nostalgia
overcasts my spill. Do they still have the floor?
Or is image the sand of picture-trillion particles?"

Facing Pollock's "Number 1. 1949" at the Los Angeles Museum of
    Contemporary Art: A Second Take

Infinitive labyrinth. World map compressed into an actional abyss.
Sand dribbled over depth's raised seams.

Pinches of earth as nodes in constellations liquefying. Ziggurat
    zigzag.
Not my being but being's bender bowled through me!

Head as a tool to decherubize Eden. Stoop & swivel.
Textures of the winter masses of aerial branches
webbing the memory of leaves. Shift to drip & densify.
A stone wall for all who seek an easel expiation!

Quicken by thinning, slow by flooding.
Divine keen of this Rorschach gale, this fly alphabet of iridescent
    mica.
To dig the rood trench, electro-wave Picasso in. May he release
    through me
the manic pistons in the mermaid's trunk!

Each brush stroke a gust from all compass points. Obstetrical secret:
overlay to reveal the interplay, the asunder ply of wonder!
Traveling white lightning shall be
guardian of the undertow, death & her lodge free progeny!

Facing Hieronymus Bosch's *Garden of Earthly Delights* in the Madrid
    Prado:

Lovers excreting pearls inside a mussel shell.
Like hermit crabs, these nudes: any interior is home.
The great regression to the primordial athanor,
the mother sea slurp & bubble of watery dark where dreaming is so
    intense it is a whirring honeycomb.

Male squadrons shovel coal into a pulsing white queen who births
    upon ignition.
A Zoa-ball in which fetuses are singing like canaries in their skeletal
    cradles.
Discombobulated rug-cutters, crowns askew, blast apart as fetuses
    turn into Katzenjammer hybrids.
                          The vision whips back into Eden:
in his vulvar side, Adam is a smoking retort of androgynous spleen.
Bumblebee kings are crouching & cooing about the manger barge:
"Just who is this Holy Ghost who impregnates from afar?"
                                Aztec culture zips in:
a ball of feathers drops on Coatlicue out sweeping—voila!
She's pregnant with Huitzilopochtli. Out squirms the king of war.

Just what is in that black testicular pod from which we've been
    drinking?
Not the keelson of creation Walt Whitman called love!
Fools have been let into our Ship of Death; a sarcophagus is its keel.
Do we dare take on our own impassioned reality?
Can we tack into the spills of infant terror mistranslated & stored?
For all artists are naked facing the ladder pointing toward the Tavern
    of the Scarlet Bagpipe.
Yet no single imagination can perform apocatastasis.
Wholeness is uterine. All roads are scabs over the wounds of diaspora.

Hear yourself whinny as you strain to toss a fruit ball to a dolphin
    performing for her supper.
The crowd roars. The fire in the circus will never be put out—
flames will destroy the giant mallards, the half-submerged earless owl,
but the crowd will continue to demand more victims for the solar maw,
for life to continue requires Aztec carnage!

The intoxications of immortality light up the switchboards when
    someone is murdered.
The furnaces of immortality are fed with the bodies of people who
    look a wee different than we do.
How does this work, Donald Rumsfeld?
Does your Reaper retreat an inch for each sixteen-year-old Iraqi boy
    snipered while out looking for food?
Men with political power are living pyramids of slaughtered others.
Bush is a Babelesque pyramid of blood-scummed steps.
The discrepancy between the literal shape & psychic veracity is nasty
    to contemplate.
Imagine a flea with a howitzer shadow
or a worm whose shade is a nuclear blaze.

December 2015–February 2016

Walking on the gym track this morning, I noticed Death's calf
in the man walking in front of me, he had on anklets & shorts,
with very long, narrow & bony white legs.
One calf, the left one, was Death's.
As I followed him around the track I could see in this calf
something under the skin moving up & down.
As I thought of worms, I noticed there were a line of little pulses.
Then, as if a gift to my attention, the calf opened to a mass of
    machinery,
tape worms sliding about rapidly, moving gears, some being cut up,
others moving through the gears.   I thought of Chaplin
& as I did, there was a whirr, many of the sliced up worms were
spit out, in a seething mass, at which point voices in my head
fired questions like:

Can't you hear the angels vomiting? Don't you see their hunched,
    shuddering backs?

14 July 2011

PHOSPHORESCENT ANGEL

Carried Hecate to the curb
& left her there, at the mercy of men
who arrive at dawn   while
still asleep   I'm turning on my own spit,
being basted, food for the gods of day.

From morn to dusk they pick me clean.
The compost will increase until once a week
I grasp her wrinkled nape & head for the curb.

Those who pull up at dawn will treat her
much more roughly than I   until
the earth   sick of our shit,
splits to reveal   her
crap-soaked hematite core.

12/24/2016

CLAYTON ESHLEMAN

WINTER BRANCHES

bereft of floral guides in grey clear sky
invoke Pollock's Aurignacian wall floor drip meanders,
for example, the 1950 #32:

embrangled masses of boughs & twigs,
ramuliferous,
vimineous.
angular auto-da-fés, sky voltage without pattern,
farrago of the subconscious mind
crossing wicker-tenuous consciousness

The day seems windless, yet the branches quaver, listless,
phantomatic Laocoon folds,
no leaves to evoke a concealed a green man—

might there be a black diviner
configured by these angular coils,
conducting, against cold obstruction,
a skeletal Giverny Mass?

Gnarl embroidery, static maelstrom,
what dying calls its own facing death...

The inalienable otherness of each, human & non-human.

The silence, the time-warped abidance
rising above these back yards...

9 January–28 February, 2017

Surely we all keep our adolescence. Surely
  it still seeks to speak. Mine has been croaking for decades.
I feed it dust. It croaks louder.
I feed it metaphor. It sings as if hypnotized by *Beowulf*.
Background is fodder, dry rot, & apocalypse,
a bent centipede folded with innocence & first alarm.
Adolescent perjuries: a doily on a State Department plate.
Dick Foltz trawling for sixteen-year-old pussy.
Is that sheer ugliness in back of our foreign policy?
I was in the backseat of his dad's car with all of them,
swigging crucifixion horror as Coca Cola mixed with sperm.
The void slips in, silvery, a glare over water-skiing lads.

23 December, 2010

The pleasure of submerging, of hunting scarves among
  the volleying winds,
of feeling out old systems Jim Hillman once took a wrench to,
safes submerged in rotting apples, the eternal post-Eden hangover of
womb dreams, as glaciers recede &
oil appears on the skin of newborns, black rouge
surfacing as if from a damaged reptilian lode.

The pleasure of palpitating one's animal slant,
the extent to which self-regard is based on the way
one treated one's pets. Who can digest
every animal soul taken in, via meat, via cuddling
the spectre of one's mom in a wire-haired romance?

I am aware that the Cro-Magnon hub can be felt at
any one turn in one's labyrinth, hub of
limestone, hub of bone, hub in which my eyes scan,
as if through a telescopic microscope,
the excoriation of human insides, flayed
nomenclatures, first signs sparkling in nebulae
no more remote than the animal parking lot in which
our billions of skeletons are aligned.
At times they shift at night in a skipping heart beat—
is water God? At the bitter conflict at the center,
where intercourse is beheading, I turn into a moth
trapped in the silk of the space in my flame.

1 Dec 2011

THE GRINDSTONE OF RAPPORT

Only through my breath do I behold this world attached to
the thread of a dream.

Yellowed intention seeps from me unintentionally.

Solar semen fills the universe: sun rays, saliva,
honey, crystal & quartzite, lutescent animals…

There has been only one real change:
the presence of being in the Upper Paleolithic.

Image-making was the unlocking of the interlocked

Imagination separation & re-spanning.

Separation created loss, loss duplicated deluge.

Paradise was the first "projective verse,"
not "over the rainbow," but: beyond the first Lethe, to
envision uterine loss on our mother-of-always: rock.

Tectiform: first "house,"   to brand a bison with
    enclosure of symbolic life.
"Roof" by which the sky is "raised."   Transcendence:
uphold the distance between kinds of being.

Who is to say that the stars are only slain animals?
May they not also be consumed plants & killed humans?
The dark is pocked with unearthly light,
night itself is sarcophagus & we, the so-called living,
    are in pause between
            closed-eye vision & primordial remove.

2015

CHAUVET, FIRST IMPRESSIONS

The depth of body.
The depth   of a hollow
    animal belly
imagination fills out to an agreeable convexity, &
the tenderness in a bear drawing
like a loom within stone.
Seesaw pitch of breath & stasis:
my heart pounding   Take Heed   halfway
up the mountain to Chauvet's entrance.
Frightened to almost be stopped within minutes of the cave.
(Olson in *Hotel Steinplatz* feeling
the World Tree give way in his giant frame).

Is that why Chauvet's interior was tinged for me
    with the rust of farewell?
Coffee outside the equipment nook
after the 40 minute climb:
4000 people, the guide Charles told us, have visited,
about 400 a year, or did he mean
about 400 will visit this year?
So I'm not that special—
    photo of the Methodist Hospital window
    the room where I was born, X'ed by my father
    in his "Baby's Book of Events".

Cradle of art?
Roar of images cascading the wall,
rows of larger-than-life lion heads voracious for
a vertical totem pole of bison heads.

90% of Chauvet is virgin floor.
One bear skull is enveloped in stalactitic casing,
a polished white sarcophagus of sorts,
with a stalagmite a foot high "growing" out of
    the cranium dome,
as if the skull sends up an opaque
    shaft of words.
10% of Chauvet appears to be metal walkway.
"charter'd Thames"   Nice to keep that much floor virgin
but it is as if this primordial labyrinth has been
    jigsawed with streets. Meaning:
no wandering, no "lost at sea" in being's immensity.
Like a huge solitary hanging fang, near the cave's end:
a Minotaur, with a drizzle of fingers,
drawn on a large feline body drawn there earlier.

Some panels boil with activity,
as if they magnetized Cro-Magnon soul,
sucked animal through Cro-Magnon bodies.
The 32,400 year old male rhino
in horn clash with maybe a female
has a fat, pointed erect phallus.
A chaos of animals, like "a paradise of poets,"
one masterly horse finger-painted in wall clay,
    shaded so carefully
to pull the outline boundaries in,
the limestone shows through—
as if nothing that special has happened since!
As if man were an afterthought of a humanimal brew
    still beating in my chest
like a wedge of lions crafting a kill.

Asking why certain spots were chosen for figures,
like asking why lightning here, not there…
Here-not-there coalesces into hermetic knots of
    wiggling anti-cores,
as if a solid helix were, this instant,
bursting into univocal lanes
(the metal walkway puns upon).

Why are you here?
right up my nose,
as if a tweezer carbon-dated, on the spot,
    a bit of my brain &
came up with the abyss's
invisible but definite bottom:
death, as a feline gush of misercordia,
beauty & affinity, lined within the notion of being.
How did I manage to walk that last 20 minutes
    up this mountain?
Why can't I get over that pounding halo of
    serpent breath,
haruspex enigma…   Breathe &
    be grateful for
the various ranges quilted within, &
the many years with Caryl.
Thought of her on that mountain side, panting…
Did her devotion & utter decency
    lift me on?

NOTE: See also the poem "Chauvet: Left Wall of End Chamber" in *Reciprocal Distillations* (Hot Whiskey Press, 2007) reprinted in *CE / The Essential Poetry (1960–2015)*. With James O'Hern, I visited Chauvet Cave with guide Jean-Marie Chauvet (one of the 1994 discoverers) on January 8, 2004. My gratitude to Dominique Baffier for arranging our visit. Excellent color photographs of the wall with the paintings addressed in my poem may be found in *Chauvet Cave / The Art of Earliest Times*, directed by Jean Clottes (The University of Utah Press, Salt Lake City, 2003).

The depths of the soul sends up flavors, vibratory flails.
Image is based on soul, & soul is in exile always because we
are never up to its down. A work of art
radios: soul exile is nigh,
tangential here to animal-clustered foliage.
Early mental travelers in a fogged
courtship with the awful miracle of unplumbable paradise.
Oh, difficulty of the soul!
                              I circle about moth gold,
flame fold. Nothing explanatory grasps what a poem senses
when integral to its irony slights, its Derrida shutters.
Bottom was paleolithically crossed by something alive,
first earth mud was lifted as an engrailing.
We will never see it again because we are its orphans.

11/26/2017

The Abbé Breuil, unlike Ezekiel lying in dung,
on his back on stone, copying the nearly invisible in Combarelles
not to raise man to a vision of the infinite, but to lower
the infinite to a vision of the visible in man,
the lines of what in time man has hidden, nearly invisible scrapings,
silex sortilege rainbowed through limestone—
where the infinite comes up against
the ungraspability of words, nets of utterance that,
like mammoths crossing, in lines can be expressed…

I am envisioning Breuil with candle,
inaccurate at times, his mind's cassock only partially unwrapped by
the way the "pre" of prehistory is visibly
invisible in something his hand   reached up for,
        a seamless impurity.

                                        12/20/2017

ROBES

"And it was only the robe that drove him on,
a vision of the inland sea, which is called the Gull-robe,
gorgeous, of white feathers emblazoned with stars & moons,
the lovely garment every loved woman wears, of midnight-blue &
    silks,
in which a light streams for all who ride away into the darkness
carrying the torches of imaginative love,
the softness & perfection of loved desire."

This stanza from "The Book of Niemonjima" written in Blooming-
ton, Indiana, 1965. In 1963, Paul Blackburn enclosed a photo of a gull
standing on a rock in a letter to me in Kyoto, writing under the image:
Dear Clay, Never look a gull in the eye, love Paul. That admonition
puzzled me, for I knew that Paul loved to look & watch, & that some
of his most characteristic poems had him sitting someplace, on a street
bench or in a park, watching what was going on around him. So in
1963 I did not pick up the gull wall connection to be found in a 1960
Blackburn poem, "The Purse-seine":

    We cannot look one another in the eye,
                             that frightens, easier to face
    the carapace of monster crabs along the beach . The empty
    shell of death was always easier to gaze upon
    than to look into the eyes of the beautiful killer . Never
                        look a gull in the eye)

Today, at the NYC Metropolitan Museum Plains Indian Art exhibition:
Mythic Bird robe
geo-mythic strength,
beak detached from round head

To wear the buffalo:
Cro-Magnon vespers.
To paint on hide
instead of cave stone—
out under sun
instead of deep in the mother vortex
as the Plains filled with white invaders

Did Cro-Magnon wear hide robes?
No signs of them on cave walls.
The geo-matriarchal scheme:
by mother rake I am swept, piled,
as embers I go up.

On these Plains the cave is carried on body,
warrior skirmish decked in robe-folds

(our tuxedo a cartoon of hide spirit drapery)

Otter skin bag—
the wrinkled head: pulverized presence.
Quills of a spirit's scarred healing.
Eyes immobile as if frozen.
Carrier for human stuff
infused with solar synaesthesia.

ORPHEUS IN LASCAUX

The Lascaux Pit's visionary scene is much more formidable & larger
than I had anticipated before climbing down a narrow 16 foot ladder
to it in May 1997. Around 6 and a half feet in length the scene pos-
sesses its wall space with black, aggressive, calligraphic strokes. In
reproductions it often appears cramped, with a bird-headed man, a
wounded bison, & a rhinoceros done in a puerile, "primitive" fashion.
As I stood before them, these figures struck me as commanding as the
images of bison & horses in the Rotunda & Axial Galleries above.
The manganese glistens; the six dots right behind the incomplete
rhinoceros's anus shine, as if still wet!

The bird-headed man, his bird-topped staff, & these six dots were
possibly the original figures on the Pit's wall. This naked figure with
an erection & outstretched handless four-fingered arms appears to be
in a trance & I propose that he may be the first indication of the pres-
ence of Orpheus in our world. The bird perched on the staff right
below his right arm is staring at (given their placement) the six turds,
probably the first marks made in one of the terminal areas of Lascaux
(another, also marked by six dots, being at the end of the Chamber of
the Felines, the area farthest from the cave's entrance). The Pit's turd
dots are directly over an inverted V-like fissure in the wall that widens
into a small but gaping hole going nowhere.

The Greek poet Simonides wrote that "above Orpheus's head flutter
innumerable birds." One European root for "Orpheus" offers "or-n"
or "erne" from old English earn, or eagle. A second suffixed form is
the Greek "ornis," the stem of "ornith," *bird* (ornithology).

It should also be noted that one of the two sorcerer-like figures engraved on the wall of the Apse indirectly over the Pit appears to be a human figure inside a dried grass costume, whose head area contains two eyes & a one-eyed bird's head. Known as "The Big Sorcerer" this figure also seems to be wearing a witch-like hat! There seems to be two bird shamans in this area of Lascaux.

The historical Orpheus appears to have been conceived in a Thracian cave during the 6th century BC. As the son of Apollo, he enchanted animals as well as birds, & as one of the Argonauts, his lute was "strung with poets' sinews." After the Bacchae tore him to pieces, his shamanic head, which Philostratus wrote ended up in Lesbos, continued to deliver spells & incantations. Pythagoras wrote that the poet must not tear apart this god within himself. Orpheus's relationship to the underworld was confirmed when he descended into Hades, that unfathomed mine of souls, in an attempt to bring Eurydice back to earth.

The bison above and to the right of the Orphic bird-man is the most difficult figure to contextualize in this visionary scene. Its head is unnaturally lowered with both of its horns pointing at the man's elongated torso, & its front legs have been pulled back to the extent that it could not stand; its beard, neck and withers appear to be unconnected to its head (which can also be seen as a horse head facing in the opposite direction). A spear laid across its anus points diagonally to the left crossing the animal's distended belly in front of its disgorged intestines. Some of these peculiar aspects may be intended to emphasize that the bison is dead. Unlike the quite alive rhinoceros's flipped backward tail, the bison's tail is flipped forward—another indication of its death?

Based on the number of engravings in the Apse & Apsidole (indirectly above the Pit), & the number of lamps & tools found on the Pit's floor (more than in any other area of the cave), these two areas may have been the most visited & sacred for those who decorated Lascaux. These places quite possibly hosted workshops where tools inspired by images on the walls were fashioned.

*

NOTES: in all writings on Lascaux that I have read, the Pit is referred to as the Shaft. Since a shaft is usually identified as a passage through the floors of a building, as in an elevator shaft, I have preferred to identify this deep enclosed area as a pit.

For a more detailed reading of this scene, see the "Apse and Shaft" chapter in *Juniper Fuse.*

Orpheus is an ancient Greek legendary hero endowed with superhuman musical skills. It is said that his music & singing could not only charm the birds but also coax trees & rocks to dance. The bird-headed shamanistic male figure in the Pit scene in the Upper Paleolithic painted cave of Lascaux in the French Dordogne region may be the earliest image we have of the figure later known as Orpheus.

CLAYTON ESHLEMAN

ORPHIC ONTOLOGIES I

For Matthew Eshleman

Are you, Muse, the spume off Laussel, archaic
dust dimpled & savory that I nourish to steel myself against
the Selfhood that lays claim to all rapture?
Is your fertility still based on the blood-filled bison horn
Laussel grasps in her right hand raised slightly below her head?

Might the egg-shaped relief of a double figure near Laussel
be a Paleolithic premonition of the serpent-encircled Orphic egg?
Greeks believed that at death a man's spinal marrow
emerged from loins in serpent form.
Since bones are the framework of life,
the semen-like marrow in the skull was for centuries
thought to be the source of semen.
Thus the singing skull, the oracular skull,
an archosis going back to brain-eating Australopithecus erectus.

In every desire a uterus shelved with skulls.

I released the energy from the gateless gate of a rock face.
The wonder of inhabited nothingness bubbled & waned in me,
    microscopic doodad.
Then I heard manticores chortling with their triple band-saw
    mouths—
or was I hearing the love-songs of Max Beckmann?

Ochre dots circulating around a breast-like wall protuberance in
   Le Combel
bearing in their menstrual, apotropaic sigils the presence of
   Cro-Magnon woman
embedded so deep in collective mind
I can only wonder if planetary peril is not inscribed in image beginnings.

Is our war on animals a planetary cannibalization to reach non-existence
in a masque performed by hydrogen mountains & sulfur assassins?

The torn heaven tent draped over our lightmares.

Blake under covers at night. As if an anaconda entered as I tried to
   sleep
& wept insomnia into every shutter of my piles.

Hades is the king of remembered images.

Orpheus did bring Eurydice back. He couldn't bring her THROUGH.

To keep images in the embrace of each other & maintain the
   intercourse of their self-revealing conversations.

Is anything left of the beginning?
How about the soul's dragonfly metastases?
Or the petrified lightning rampant in a bear?

A sloth in a skin-tight body hose of drowned men.

After a vaporized storm, glassy eyes float about, burial mounds
  invading the bolted stars.

Rainer Marie Rilke to Lotte Hepner, November 8, 1915: "When a tree
blossoms death as well as life blossoms in it, and the field is full of
death, which from its reclining face sends forth a rich experience of
life, and the animals move patiently from one to another—and every-
where around us, death is at home, and it watches us out of the cracks
of things, and a rusty nail that sticks out of a plank somewhere does
nothing day and night except rejoice over death."

At the core of our Milky Way galaxy:
animal eyes in a blackish, red density of dust clouds, horns in smears
  of light.
As if life on earth is anticipated in this 300 light-years panorama.

Coitus as the earthly version of cosmic superimposition.

Sciomantic penetrations course a vineyard.

At times, I see miles of pools, piles of pumas sunning their scorpion
  sores,
four boars mating in silken anguish.

James Hillman writes: "Soul is vulnerable and suffers; it is passive and
remembers, it is water to the spirit's fire, like a mermaid who beckons
the heroic spirit into the depths of passions to extinguish its certainty.
Soul is imagination, a cavernous treasury—to use an image from St.
Augustine—a confusion and richness, both."

In sleep's porphyry mist, Daphne's lauraceous hues.

A nude asleep in a water-lily harness rotating through my breakfast.
  Drink from this tambourine.

The portentous, alpine edges in every doorway.

                                        November 15, 2015

ORPHIC ONTOLOGIES II

The essence of human power:
access to the cosmos from the heavens down to
earth & into the Cro-Magnon underworld.

Charles Olson on Wallace Stevens to Creeley, May 5, 1952: "For the
lie in Stevens, however much the pleasure in the play of words, is his
language, that, it is without rhythm because it is without passion
which is person (not personae, that further divide against mass)."

To Creeley, May 6, 1952: "We both had a sudden excitement, just now
talking, when it turns out (it was that fucking Stevens who had pro-
voked it by some line about poetry to undo dirt) O that dirty Crispin
of his—dirtier than Prufrock): those who keep themselves away from
life (again protecting a—the—pudenda) that Con said
   I don't feel any dirt
              And Christ I loved her, for, there ain't none, and those
who have it, who have this thing of original sin hung around their
cocks like a dead albatross, are of another tribe, a tribe of sin not at all
of the tribe of men
                  And it struck us both just then that what
makes communication with you so open is, that you have none of this
shit in you: you are free of that."

In the beginning was drawing, line on stone or bone,
consciousness united with its own perceptions: womb of the creative!
A totally metaphoric world, no difference between subject & object.
Dream holes: anywhere but nowhere in particular.

James Hillman: "The most distressing images in dreams and fantasies, those we shy from for their disgusting distortion and perversion, are precisely the ones that break the allegorical frame of what we think we know about this person or that, this trait of ourselves or that. The 'worst' images are thus the best, for these are the ones that restore a figure to its pristine power as a numinous person at work in the soul."

Think of this page as a phare on night's alabaster dives & cornucopian emptiness, cross-wired to the ochre of farraginous dreams.

One's place is an expanding lesion in ancestral fog. Ultimately I am, sitting here, a ghost figure crouched before a cave wall 20,000 years ago.

Pregnant abyss of the enigma of male birthing. Non-existent gestation—egg fertile only with the maggot of self.

Is our war on animals a planetary cannibalization brought about by self eating self to reach non-existence in a masque performed by hydrogen mountains & sulfur assassins?

The salmagundi of "now" & "forever" is the crucible that contains the frailty of eternity.

James Hillman: "Images are the compelling source of morality and religion as well as the conscientiousness of art." Show this to Gary Snyder [See the Winter 1996 *Paris Review* Snyder Interview].

The writhing of precision as it meets time.
Perception is the handmaiden of imagination.

Cornucopia of the sunshine forest with its anteater molecules,
a Reich bion lurking in each word
whose apogee is cratered with emptied hives.

Sun as a circumference concentrate.

It is not enough to represent, to re-
present, the present as leftovers.
Warmed up past is *forever* at our heels.

The analphabetic, orthochromatic, anti-nature of the mind when
freed of cauliflower containment.

Alive to the dead end in every observational move.

At the corner of Bukowski & Ashbery a groin helmeted with bridal
choirs.

Fingering the pluck of plumeless existence ripe with skinned heads.

A Mayan anaconda coils below Arcadia's latent still.

A stratigraphic sequence reveals its ember-work, its furnace forum
always underway. It rests in a floral nest, a leaden, still hissing egg.

James Hillman: "We have to tie terrorism to its roots in our religious
consciousness. A terrorist is the product of our education that says
that fantasy is not real, that says aesthetics is just for artists, that says
soul is only for priests, imagination is trivial or dangerous and for cra-

zies, and that reality, what we must adapt to, is the external world and that world is dead. A terrorist is a result of this whole long process of wiping out the psyche."

The greatest insult is to be pressed to
the backside of a word, whose lobes are in contact with
what the word is said to signify—a folly
(is it any wonder, then,
that people back their cradles up to their coffins
to dump in life unlived?)

To revivify my mummy, not my mommy,
but my puppet, my eidolon where Hart Crane is
a mass of strings in cross-pull to themselves.
Cross-pull or crucifixion strut,
nail-holed Hart as the mage of my abyss,
as old as Dionysus but not as old as Lascaux…

The I spoken here is not Clayton
but Being reflected by Clayton's non-existence-to-be.

The ego which absorbs all like a sponge & then is dissolved in the
   Void of the Abyss.

"It is when we have made this leap or jump across the Abyss—and only then—that we know that we are not… At that moment we real-ize that we are void, that void is subjectivity, and that subjectivity is us—not us as individual selves but us as all sentient beings, not as any sort of sentient being but as sentient *being* as such. That is the nega-

CLAYTON ESHLEMAN

tive way… that is why we must know that we are not in order that we may understand in what manner we can be." (Wei Wu commenting on Han Shan's words).

Poussin's satyr-scape is no more.
The anointing of the dead Adonis. No more.
Pan's shadow as leafy quilts. Psychic clouds boiling westward. No
  more.
Blind Orion searching for the risen sun. No more.

2017

MARGINALIA TO WESTON LA BARRE'S *MUELOS*

Today I have placed my mother's bones in anatomical position.
I have explored the semen in these bones.
In her skull I have discovered the cobweb of myself,
   my brain in futurity, &
I have eaten the guardian spider that in a carbon mask
   offered itself to me
once the bones were assembled.

First I severed her legs, & then drained her spinnerets.
Each of her eight eyes watched me, in stare with Rilke's
There is no place that does not see you.
There is no place in which you do not spend your manly marrow.
But between your genitals & your mind there are only
   exploded bridges
                Alchuringa, impinge,
open your foramen magnum to me,
let me see the oldest ones in brain with the recent ones,
let me taste the male muelos, to know it is as close &
as distant as worm tangles exposed while clearing away
   winter leaves.
This knot, forever loose, slimy, other, of Medusa, boneless,
this taste of blackboard blank, writhing keelson, horned worm,
my mind is your ball-court, the ball is named
Blood Girl, or Daisy, solar facing circle jerk.
Attached to my own horse neck I sing my own fruit,
I am embalmed & displayed in my chest,
I have taken my own head, I control my spirit!
   Cleaned out   gilded   holy
                apotropaic gargoyle,

thrust out tongue upon which language
coils,   it now in I,   I now in it,
      black egg, compost covenant.
   My worms advance waving antlers,
   each drools a Dordogne from each tip.

Skull & crossbones: the double-penised seed moor of Death
nailed to the immortality
magnum in the heart of man. Marrow whiskey.
To your health, skull!
              And then I shifted on my cob
& flew into bowl. At the head of my stream
to know my jaw knee. Cerebrum cereal:
          fetus-femur-fecunda-femina.

To honor these vitalities I have reassembled my mother bones.
She is infinite.   My semen finite.
I, the zero sum. She, the milky. How now,
that eternity has flown,
   replenish the poem's infinity?

You must procure at least one human head.
That woman impregnates man must be revealed.
Man must become a femur-fecunda-fetus-femina *flame*

I obtain my masculinity from another man.
But I hold it—this bound pussy willow bunch—
to the cunt of a masked sow.
      Will you ignite, clandestine reader?
or will the pronouns crackle & fail?
Will the associating end up in pun?

If we add to this the fact that a world-wide
primitive belief is that masculinity is a commodity
(finite in nature) to be obtained from another male:
we have an amazing double bind:

I protect myself from the dead by killing;
This action also offers me my male identity.
By killing other men, I impotentize the dead & potentize my life.

A tree filled with sago grubs. An ass filled with brains.

When head hunting was suppressed
among the Toraja of Celebes there was intense anxiety
    lest the ancestral spirits,
no longer fed with a "harvest" of enemy heads,
might eat the villagers themselves.

Does war, then, exist as soul food for the dead?

ALCHURINGA TIME

Looking into the telescope of the night,
with its vehicular cinders, its naked sea butterflies,
I contemplate the composted humanity
under me, or
of self, so latent as to be a dwarf lantern,
to realize what the male head means to my Sepik layers,
to kill so as to amass souls, soul strength of others,
& to dine on brain, & the cave-like
interior of the bone.
                              At the juncture of Rumsfeld
    & Yorunomado, souls provide
supernatural power, immunity
                                        from death.
How deeply is the worm of immortality is
aghast in me, a flicker gourd, something firing in
my vegetal flavors.
                              To bring all of this close,
to reveal & embed,
to be at thick with my self.

In world obliteration, caught up
    in the piston of a drive
to wear a semen bone through my nose,
to be vermilion in a cloud of gnats,
a force amidst the talking trees—
how thin rationality & shoes appear
set beside animistic gore,
                              soul-driven blindness to
the reciprocal, the "sane"—

Inside the soul bone I munch, suck, & draw.
I am a kind of ant, many-legged, with a head packed with
   holy robes,   life
grinds up in me, the silex between my fingers
cuts to the bone my tweezered lust to
   live & to live & to see women
as through a periscope: are they wrestling anacondas?
Or moon slivers, metate-bent filaments,
                              mothers of the peccary
   into which the sun ejaculates its lightning?

                  Paralyzed by finiteness,
I hover the semen stored in testicular vats.
Everytime I spurt, the trees flash me their vaginas,
barked gates into soul-racked realms...

So I am here, an old man stretched out under his belly,
while As If focuses & refocuses in the night's
   magnanimous lens... Now or never,

to build into the poem a packed humanity
with abysses below the furnaces of reason,
in which the 21st century, like a baleful shark eye, rimmed with fire,
gazes upon its hideous justifications,
feels warmth for its wounded, then wounds them again
as if we men were, at the precipice of the cosmic vagina,
fighting, jacking off, & dancing, all at once, to impede
the feminine from closing over. That we might face,
among the splotched karate of our contact

the mirrors of immortality...

                           Into these abysses

    to plant imaginal spannings.

                                             8 August 2010

I stand in our second floor bathroom at 4 AM looking out the window
at The First United Methodist Church of Ypsilanti across Washtenaw
Road from our house. I am looking at its two main door lights
through our leafless red maple tree. The branches demethodize the
lights so that they become eyes of a creature whose head is structured
by the branchwork. A world tree? A presence not of church or tree, a
creature whose eyes emit pagan light. An *axis mundi* specter, is it? Or
glyph in, & out, of present time? Into what face do I stare into own
mind? Creature face? Branchwork head. Hart Crane's suicide
sorghum passes through & holds, here, as a reoccurring moment *of
night*—is this the face of the head *of night*? What night is making of
me as I transform church into what is behind or under it? A spirit tree
head, a hagazussa?

Why don't you risk weather-roping a raft to the stain of being 83?
The pattern guide is oblivion spell, words no longer safe from sleep's
    connect to not being here.
I'm wondering how Pollock would've dripped 4:10 AM when & if
    the spell of vanish had lifted the octopus out of the modesty of
    knowing nothing of around-the-corner——love?

      By-stream in
      lie-strain,
          to lie now in
the flow of no, make "no" big,
scratch your "are" as if in Combarelles. be first as you last,
     stand here facing the trace of 83 bottom up…

Bolster, game the maze of no longer knowing what from whether.
Isn't it time to forget time, to inspect your *origin*
since no word will instill a savior path.

I write the risk & randomness of fixture now,
now as a timed spar
atoss with cracked fouls.

Think of the page as a wall
on which to draw through
aging's havoc a signaling sphere
  atmosphere
        phare,
            a lighthouse on
                night's alabaster
                    dives & monoliths,
night's cornucopian emptiness, what dreaming
attempts to stifle & to rid of bilge
—oh no,   night is
cross-wired to every glance of my life,
of a density parked
then abandoned with pets in the zoo of tall years,
the boles & excrescence of
all I've touched.
    The problem of saying all:
moles gnawing through each word
    as it appears—
broken pylons of my strife gain.

November 2018

POLLEN ARIA

The dark is pocked with sarcophagi.
We, the dreaming, are in pause between
closed-eye vision & primordial remove.

To ring out of dew a blackness packed with geyser & alabaster
rippling with millepedel pennants,
the Cro-Magnon sensation of an open dream.

One is always in birth delivery until a hybrid transformation is
    performed.
Thus shamanism responds to a grand & ancient need.

Weston La Barre: "The idea that a singing head or skull could
shamanize as an oracle long after its owner's death, as both Virgil and
Ovid asseverate, suggests the immense antiquity of the old Stone Age
skull cult."

When I was a womb passenger
I could see daddy fussing about the ring,
the sole spectator at my title match.
"Punch placenta," he huffed.
He's bet 20 bulls I'd come out swinging
with my brain hooded like a whelk,
with a marrow stare.

So I asked Bruce Conner:
does a fetus have the Kervorkian right to not exit the womb?

How trellis this contest of life versus no?
Ponder the bridal scree?
Wander a woodpecker abandon
by brain-drilling the family beech?

Poetry is the cosmogonic pupa in the chrysalis of day.

According to Gerald Massey, the earliest forms of human speech
resembled the clicking of the kaf ape.

Nothing explanatory grasps the Orphic radar of a poem
when it performs its pollen aria.

Now I recall that coalbin mouth before which my father positioned me
freshly-cut switch in hand. I glimpsed Hart Crane in that bin,
the oriflamme & astral kale rampant in his eyes.
He murmured: become an air octopus in a tentacle tryst with clouds.

Is the poet archetypally entangled with a daemon whose face,
like a malformed vagina, appeared on certain Cro-Magnon cave
    walls?

"You will commit a horrible crime—
you will be put away for the rest of your life—
this is the payment for having jettisoned your background."

Daemon babble. Don't tell me you haven't experienced it
as you washed dishes, or tried to shit.

My closest glimpse of divinity: 30,000 B.P. say, when ur-shamanism
envisioned an exchange between bison & human beings.

Arctic hysteria—
possibly fundamental to shamanism.
No potion needed.
the novice learns to control his hysteria,
becomes its driver, ecstatic release,
springboard for "the journey."

Charred girders call out to us. Screens of a stirring.
Parasites in sponge-like textures. Afterlife of the gone.

Finnegan's Wake: end again wakes.

When did the end first wake?

"Our little boy is born this day at 10:50 A.M. His Daddy seeing him
enter this old world. A little Clayton Jr. our dream at last realized and
our prayers answered. Thank God for it all."

As a pupa in the chrysalis of day, it takes a lifetime to gauge the
contraries in the arc of night.

There is more Orpheus in Betty Carter than in Harold Bloom.

Absence has more specter caviar than any other word.
Absence is not mine, nor to be mined as "thine."
The womb: its mortal joke.

When the poem's stow-away potential connects to its pump & locks,
throttles release their anaconda mainline to
what a moment ago was merely a mirror
in which Hart Crane's ghost was staring at the marigold

drift in inspiration's latent mire.
Now seams yield their undertow & being 83 no longer flaunts
an unrealizable bell tower charge...

We are Servants of the Pivot on which all things turn.

June 2017–March 2018

INTERVIEW WITH CLAYTON ESHLEMAN
[IRAKLI QOLBAIA]

Irakli Qolbaia: *Your poem,* Short Story, *begins with "Begin with this: the world has no origin", and yet, there seems to be, in your poetry, a constant quest for origin — personal origins, origins of imagination / of poetry. There is even a Blakean "character", Origin, in your early poem of the same title (referring to Cid Corman and his 'origin'?). Could you talk about that sense of origin in your poetry, and more specifically, about your origins as a poet?*

Clayton Eshleman: My relationship to origins has been multifaceted. I think my first engagement was hearing at 16 years old on a 45 RPM record the bebop pianist Bud Powell play his improvisation on the standard tune "Tea for Two." I listened to Powell's version again and again trying to grasp the difference between the standard and what Powell was doing to and with it. Somehow an idea vaguely made its way through: you don't have to play someone else's melody—you can improvise (how?), make up your own melody line! WOW— really? You mean I don't have to repeat my parents? I don't have to "play their melody" for the rest of my life? Later I realized that Powell had taken a trivial song and transformed it into an imaginative structure. While reading the Sunday newspaper comics on the living-room floor was probably my first encounter, as a boy, with imagination, Powell was my first experience, as an adolescent, with the force of artistic presence and certainly the key figure involved in my becoming a poet when I was 23 years old.

Soon after starting to try to write poetry at Indiana University in 1958 I found Cid Corman's poetry journal called *Origin* in the library. I began a correspondence with Cid and when I was living in Kyoto, Japan, in 1962, I went to the coffee shop where Cid, also living in Kyoto at the time, could be found every evening. For a couple of years I watched him edit *Origin* and learned a lot about translating poetry from him. Corman was the first American translator of the great German poet Paul Celan and, while in Kyoto, as my poetic apprenticeship project, I decided to translate César Vallejo's *Poemas humanos* into English.

During this period I worked on Vallejo most afternoons downtown in another Kyoto coffee shop called Yorunomado (the word means "night window" in English). In the only poem I completed to any real satisfaction while living in Japan, I envisioned myself as a kind of angel-less Jacob wrestling with a figure who possessed a language the meaning of which I was attempting to wrest away. I lose the struggle and find myself on a seppuku (or suicide) platform in medieval Japan, being commanded by Vallejo (now playing the role of an overlord) to disembowel myself. I do so, imaginatively-speaking, cutting the ties to my "given" life and releasing a daemon I named Yorunomado who until that point (my vision told me) had been chained to an altar in my solar plexus. Thus at this point the fruits of my struggle with Vallejo were not a successful literary translation but an imaginative advance in which a third figure emerged from my intercourse with the text. Thus death and regeneration = seppuku and the birth of Yorunomado, or a breakthrough into what might be called sacramental existence.

While Bud Powell and Yorunomado (via Vallejo) provided brief, if essential, adventures with origin, the crucial event after leaving Japan in 1964 was my 1974 discovery of Upper Paleolithic, or Cro-Magnon, cave art in southwestern France. My wife Caryl and I had, at the suggestion of a friend, rented an apartment in a farm house in the Dordogne countryside and after visiting some of these Ice Age caves I was completely caught up in the deep past. This grand transpersonal realm (without a remaining history or language) was about as far away from my background as could be, and I revisited and researched the painted caves throughout the late 1970s, 1980s, and 1990s, becoming the first poet anywhere to do what the poet Charles Olson called "a saturation job" on the origins of art as we know it today. To follow poetry back to Cro-Magnon metaphors not only hits real bedrock—a genuine back wall—but gains a connection to the continuum during which imagination first flourished. My growing awareness of the caves led to the recognition that, as an artist, I belong to a pre-tradition that includes the earliest nights and days of soul-making. Wesleyan University Press published my book, a study composed of both poetry and prose, *Juniper Fuse: Upper Paleolithic Imagination & the Construction of the Underworld*, in 2003.

IQ: *Clayton, there are many possible questions contained in your response and I would like to come back to several of them at later points; but at this point I wish to ask about the American poetry scene at the time of your decision to become a poet. You mention the year 1958, as a sort of starting point for you — in two years Donald Allen's* New American Poetry *was to come out. Can you talk about that moment, as well as that informal, but interconnected (it seems to me) movement that was afoot at the time you started? You mention Olson and Corman; could you talk about other poets who were important to you, older or your generation? You talk about Vallejo, as a master poet; who were some initial American masters? Is it possible to talk about what that wave of New American Poetry (generally / personally for you) represented?*

CE: In 1957 I took a course in 20th century American poetry at Indiana University in Bloomington, Indiana with Professor Robert G. Kelly. I was an undergraduate senior majoring in Philosophy at the time. We studied mainly early 20th century poets and I recall writing a term paper on Robinson Jeffers' long poem "Roan Stallion."

The following year I met the graduate student and poet Jack Hirschman and his wife Ruth. The Hirschmans had come to Indiana

University from New York City where they knew the young poets Robert Kelly and Jerome Rothenberg. The Hirschmans were also aware of a number of major 20th century European poets (Lorca, Breton, Rilke, for example) and they introduced me to many of the poets I am still reading today. Jack and Ruth ran a poetry recital club called Babel, and I gave my first poetry program there by reading translations of St.-John Perse. It was at this time that I also discovered the poetry journal *Origin* in the university library, and became aware of poets like Allen Ginsberg (whose poem *Howl* published in 1956 was notoriously popular at this time), and Charles Olson, Robert Duncan, and Paul Blackburn whose writings also began to be published in the 1950s. At this time I also found the poetry of Pablo Neruda and César Vallejo in a Latin American poetry anthology and began to inspect the translations with bilingual dictionaries (I was shocked to find how inaccurately a lot of the poetry had been translated and I think that awareness was crucial in my later becoming a translator of Neruda, Vallejo, Aimé Césaire and Antonin Artaud). This was the epoch when thousands of young Americans were "on the road" and in the summer of 1958 I hitchhiked to Mexico, a journey that inspired my subsequent years spent in Japan and France. While in Kyoto from 1962 to 1964, I read all of William Blake's poetry and struggled through the jungle of his long prophetic poems like *The Four Zoas, Milton: A Poem*, and *Jerusalem*. Without the inspiration from tackling Blake's writing (I once passed out in Kyoto while reading *The Book of Urizen*) I do not think I would have had the courage to birth Yorunomado.

All of the poets mentioned above, along with Walt Whitman, Emily Dickinson, William Carlos Williams, Hart Crane, Gary Snyder, Adrienne Rich, have informed my sense of what poetry is and what it can be. Of all of these poets I think Hart Crane has meant the most to me over the decades. Poems like "Lachrymae Christi" and "The Wine Menagerie" stopped me in my tracks in the way that some of Blake did. I was being asked to stretch to accommodate an uncommon sense of things that I was intuitively convinced was not nonsense or pointlessly obscure. Crane's metaphoric shifts recall Powell's pell-mell bebop riffs or Soutine's earthquake rumba landscapes.

Here are a few comments on other poets I have mentioned, all of whom have been very important to me.

Since the 1950s, when he read his poems about the Native American trickster Coyote in San Francisco when Allen Ginsberg read Part One of *Howl,* Gary Snyder has been developing a sensual landscape-attuned poetry of change and becoming that in the light of our current awareness of planetary potential and doom has become a clearing in American consciousness. It presents itself as ruggedly and thoroughly as monumental Chinese Sung Dynasty landscape painting in a context of interconnectedness involving lore, research, meditation, and a range of living and mythical companions. *Mountains And Rivers Without End* (1996) was Snyder's 16th book, 138 pages of text, 39 poems in 4 sections or movements. This work was struck off a Sung Dynasty scroll painting as, scene by scene, it unfurls, redirecting Whitman's "adhesive love" from solely human comradeship to a comradely display that includes Artemisia and white mountain sheep. Snyder adheres to the Buddhistic principle of emptiness: there is no self, everything we see and are is empty. Thus the absence of the sensitive or tormented psychological subject in his poetry. To overturn 2000 years of Christian dominion over "unchristian" nature, the scale of values had to be massively rebalanced. *Mountains And Rivers Without End* was the first major Western poem to sweepingly foreground the natural world from a Buddhistic perspective and, without cynicism, to present civilization on a sharply diminished scale.

Robert Kelly is probably the most prolific American poet of the 20th and (so far) 21st century, being the author of over seventy collections of poetry, several novels, four works of short fiction, and two theoretical/critical books. Kelly is inventive in the way that Picasso was: he can improvise intelligently and imaginative on anything that strikes his ear, heart, or gaze. Kelly thinks of the poet as a scientist of holistic understanding. Guy Davenport has written: "No American poet except perhaps Wallace Stevens has his sense of balance in a line. What Eliot and Pound slaved over Kelly seems to have an innate gift for balancing out. He has the Chinese sense of bringing diverse things together into a stark symbol, and is happiest when he himself can't quite see the meaning of the sign he's made. I should think he would be interesting to the philosophers (had we any), for he seems to me to be a man determined to think deeply and carefully about Being itself (perhaps the one subject that pervades his poetry)."

Jerome Rothenberg's *Khurbn* (1989) is the great middle-length (40 pages) poem of our times; it takes place with a handful of other poems of similar length and scope, such as Aimé Césaire's *Notebook of a Return to the Native Land* or Vladimir Holan's *A Night with Hamlet*. The Jewish agony in the Nazi killing centers has been researched, testified to, and documented: *Khurbn* is the first American poem I know of to engage this agony emotionally, intellectually, and imaginatively. It pulls Adorno's "After Auschwitz, there can be no poetry" inside out, to read: "After Auschwitz, there is only poetry." Such a revisioning charges all poets everywhere to consider to what extent poetry itself is the language of the one hundred fifty million "violently departed" of the 20th century. *Khurbn* is precisely personal, horrifying, tender and structurally astute. Hearing Rothenberg read it several decades ago, I felt the eels of the brutalized, invisible for so many years, begin to move under my skin.

From 1996 until her death in 2012, Adrienne Rich and I wrote to each other regularly and exchanged poems in progress. In the summer of 1999, she wrote to me: "I am trying to imagine a poetics of absolute resistance which has critical resistance as its stable field yet can invoke many kinds of bending of language, but which does not depend for its testimony of resistance, simply on bending the language. A poetics that would be, both in spirit and method, resistant to the calculated destabilizations of content and context of our time—language proceeding from an indignant, outraged, undomesticated consciousness that is torqued and fired so that it indents that consciousness indelibly into the page." Rich has also written: "Self-trivialization, contempt for women, misplaced compassion, addiction; if we could purge ourselves of this quadruple poison, we would have minds and bodies more poised for the act of survival and rebuilding" and "Art means nothing if it simply decorates the dinner table of power which holds it hostage."

IQ: *Every careful reader of your work, I trust, will recognize the points you share with the poets you have so carefully considered above. But about Gary Snyder you write about "the absence of the sensitive or tormented psychological subject in his poetry". I have a belief that one of the major (often devastating) forces of your poetry has been the refusal to empty the poem completely of the sensitive and tormented self. Even in your poems directly concerned with the Upper Paleolithic, the self is present. In this I think your writing might be closer to the poets you have translated — Vallejo, Artaud, Césaire, Holan — and that the personal "darkness in the heart" should be ever present, no matter what transpersonal depths the poem might reach. Do you think this an accurate view of a certain aspect of your work? If so, could you comment on the necessity for the poet to be "the other", but only at the cost of drilling through himself?*

CE: I disagree that, to quote you, "personal darkness in the heart should be ever present, no matter what transpersonal depths the poem might reach." I want the blackness in the heart of man to be engaged as part of my primary stabilizations and concentrations, but I do not want it to rule. The imaginative world that I have attempted to create includes my twenty-five year research via the Ice Age painted caves of southwestern France on the origin of image-making, a number of poems on such artists as Caravaggio, Soutine, Leon Golub, Unica Zűrn and Hieronymus Bosch, and book-length translation projects including César Vallejo, Aimé Césaire, Antonin Artaud, Michel Deguy, Bei Dao, Vladimir Holan, and José Antonio Mazzotti. While I seek to build an atmosphere of political awareness into much of what I write, I realize that being beholden to an agenda can be as undermining to imagination as self-censorship. I primarily agree with Wyndham Lewis's view that the basis of art is that of clearing new ground in consciousness. Unless poets stave off and admit at the same time, keeping open to the beauty and the horror of the world while remaining available to what their perceptivity and subconscious provide them with, one is pretty much left with an unending "official verse culture."

Gary Snyder became in his twenties a life-long Zen Buddhist and he believes that religion is a central part of his psychological/spiritual being. In an interview in the Winter 1996 *Paris Review,* he said: "I don't think art makes a religion. I don't think it helps you teach your children how to say thank you to the food, how to view questions of truth and falsehood, or how not to cause pain or harm to others. Art can certainly help you explore your own consciousness and your own mind and your own motives, but it does not have a program to do that... I think that art is very close to Buddhism and can be part of Buddhist practice, but there are territories that Buddhist psychology and Buddhist philosophy must explore, and that art would be foolish to try to do."

I was raised in Indianapolis in a Presbyterian household. My father was a deacon in the nearby Fairview Presbyterian Church, and my mother sang in the choir there. I never had any interest in religion and when I discovered poetry I realized that this would be my life commitment and that I did not require any additional philosophy or religion to help me realize what I wanted to accomplish. I have a negative view of religion, not only for humankind in general but specifically for artists. I think religion acts as a governor on the imaginative auto and that poets who become religious in their 40s or 50s do so at the risk of compromising their imaginative focus and energies. From time to time I have speculated that Gary Snyder is potentially a wilder man than he has allowed himself to be. At the same time I recognize that his background and sensibility are very different from my own and that his accomplishments as a poet and naturalist are extraordinary. Unlike writers who become religious as part of some sort of midlife crisis, Gary Snyder's Buddhism appears to have taken root during his early 20s when he was a timber scaler and fire lookout and his masterpiece that I mentioned earlier is part of a long and daily meditative practice out of which that poem was generated and designed.

IQ: *I quote, once more, Gary Snyder from your response, that in relation to art / religion "there are territories [...] that art would be foolish to try to [explore]." Do you think there are territories that art would be foolish to explore? Should the poem not be open to everything?*

CE: I don't know what Gary has in mind by that claim, which to this day appears questionable, even naïve to me. I wish that Eliot Weinberger, the interviewer, has challenged that assertion. If the poet and Buddhist Gary Snyder knows of such "territories" that Buddhist psychology and philosophy "must explore" it would appear that Snyder himself should explore them. "Foolish" is the troubling word here.

IQ: *Can we dwell on some of this for a little longer?*

I wanted to clear up my ideas about the "darkness" I referred to. I think there is the presence of radical image and thought in your poetry and this makes me think of your description of a certain kind of poet as the "the conductor of the pit", not of the orchestra. This I understood as your command that the poet (and poem) be concerned with the unconscious, unknown, uncharted. In the book of the same name, besides the poets you already mentioned (Vallejo, Artaud, Césaire, Holan) there was also Rimbaud. I also thought that another poet who could qualify as a conductor of the pit is Lautréamont. In your essay (from Companion Spider*), you quoted Bachelard: "there is 'a need to animalize that is at the origins of imagination. The first function of imagination is to create animal forms.'"*

Could you comment on your interest in that "pit", as well as the motive of animalizing (oneself? imagination?) as important in your body of work? I also thought that your relation to the hybrid, the "pit", darkness, or the "animal", have taken a new, deeper function since you started exploring the caves and what you call "Upper Paleolithic Imagination".

CE: My primary belief concerning poetry is that it is about the extending of human consciousness, creating a symbolic consciousness that in its finest moments overcomes the dualities in which the human world is cruelly and eternally, it seems, enmeshed. Here I think of Paul Tillich's words: "A life process is the more powerful, the more non-being it can include in its self-affirmation, without being destroyed by it." Affirmation is only viable when it survives repeated immersions in negation. The problem of focusing at large on brutality and filth is that in doing so symbolic consciousness is flattened out by agit-prop and poetically-disguised journalism. I want the blackness in the heart of mankind to be engaged as part of my primary stabilizations and concentrations, but I do not want it to rule. I see it as an important aspect, no more, of the imaginative world I am attempting to create.

I have come to believe that the "I," that selva of the self, along with its chauffeur, the ego, should be opened up and explored in what might be identified as the antiphonal flow, in Northrop Frye's words, "of a bicameral mind in which something else supplants consciousness."

When I proposed to forget the orchestra and conduct the pit, I had in mind not only the subconscious but the Ice Age realm of the decorated caves. I wrote the poem "Deeds Done and Suffered by Light" in northern Italy in 1979 when I was about five years into my twenty-five year "saturation job" on the Upper Paleolithic underworld. You mention "animalizing oneself." My thinking concerning the origin and elaboration of cave image making began with an intuition while visiting the Combarelles cave just outside of Les Eyzies-de-Tayac in the French Dordogne: that it was motivated by a crisis in which Cro-Magnon people began to separate the animal out of their about-to-be human heads and to project it onto cave walls as well as onto a variety of portable tools and weapons often made out of the animals themselves. In other words, that the liberation of what might be called the autonomous imagination came from within as a projective response on the part of those struggling to differentiate themselves from, while being deeply bonded to, the animal. This would be more like a deanimalization than an animalization.

The separating out of the animal as a formative function of Cro-Magnon imagination indicated, on a daily, practical level, the increasing separation between human and animal domains. I conjecture that this separation was brought about in part by action-at-a-distance weapons (the spear, the spear-thrower, the harpoon, and probably the bow and arrow). Shamanism, or what might be more accurately termed proto-shamanism, may have come into being as a reactionary swerve from this separation continuum, to rebind human being to the fantasy of that paradise that did not exist until the separation was sensed.

In the poem in which I urge conduction of the pit I also write: "Hanged Ariadne giving birth in Hades is the rich black music in mother's tit." To integrate Hades (the first version of which was surely those ancient decorated caves) would be to assimilate subconscious information and patterns, via dreams, fantasies, slips of the tongue, and the recognition of impulsive behavior. Were every American man to get up in the morning and state out loud: "I am a potential killer and am responsible for everything that I do and that happens to me today"—and mean it, America might become less lethal. I attempted to deal with the potential killer in me near the end of my poem "Coils" (in the book, *Coils*, 1973). I let my darkest specter speak. When I read that poem in poetry readings in the mid-70s, I put a paper bag over my head with eye slits (a kind of cartoon of a Ku Klux Klan hood) when I read that section. Audiences must have thought I was crazy. Which in that speech I was.

IQ: *I think that the quotation from Northrop Frye is very important for understanding some of the directions you (as well as some others, close to you) seem to have taken in your poetic practice.*

You have reinforced my belief that darkness and the pit are related to the unconscious as well as (and in your case, probably more importantly) to the cave, cave-art, the Upper Paleolithic. This means that no matter what negativity may need to enter the poem, that darkness is mainly a positive, affirmative force related to the imagination and the extension of consciousness. Could you explain a little more how you "entered the cave"; how your "saturation job" began and how did this actual, physical practice of cave exploration become the principal fire-source of your poetry?

CE: The most complete response to this question is in my essay, "The Back Wall of Imagination: Notes on the Juniper Fuse project," to be found in my book *Archaic Design* (Black Widow Press, 2007). In the spring of 1974 we rented a furnished apartment in a farmhouse outside of Les Eyzies-de-Tayac in the French Dordogne, and soon after moving in we met the archeologist H.L. Movius Jr who had been doing research on sites near Les Eyzies for decades. Movius arranged for us to visit the original Lascaux cave (which had been closed to the public since 1963; in 1974, groups of up to five people were allowed in the cave for forty-five minutes four days a week). The guide, Jacques Marsal (one of the original discoverers of Lascaux in 1940), made us all wait in total darkness at the entrance to the Rotunda (having passed through three steel doors and having cleansed our shoe soles in a formalin solution tray). He walked away and after a minute or so turned on the muted lights. Four immense aurochs, at once moving swiftly yet static, appeared, occupying nearly sixty feet of a curving, crystal-white wall space. Across and below them, as if sprinkled there, moving in different directions, were small horses and deer. All of us were spellbound. I think that "moment of moments" sounded something in me that I could only respond to and realize through the writing of a book.

To begin to write into what I had experienced in such caves as Lascaux, Combarelles, and Font-de-Gaume entailed mounting a research project from scratch, and undertaking a poetic investigation that ended up spanning twenty-five years. While I had other projects during this period—poems not associated with prehistory, a translation of César Vallejo's book, *Trilce*, the essays collected in *Antiphonal Swing*, and editing *Sulfur* magazine for 19 years—the caves were the overarching preoccupation project. Ideally, every poet should undertake at least one big investigative project that brings into poetry materials that have previously not been a part of it. This is one way that we keep our art fresh and not diluted with variations played on tried and true themes. The investigative project also makes one responsible for a huge range of materials, the assimilation of which goes way beyond the concerns of the personal lyric.

Caryl and I initially went to France at the point when I had worked through my apprenticeship to poetry—in *Indiana* (1969), *Altars* (1971), and *Coils* (1973)—years of self-confrontation involving an excavation, at times ruthless, of my Indiana background, in effect, my given life, including its racist, Christian, and sexist values. In 1973, I was hungry for an alternative to myself. Going to the Dordogne the following spring was utter serendipity. I was suddenly faced with an ancient transpersonal world, one that is still, decade after decade (starting for the most part at the turn of the 20th century), revealing the shards, as it were, of its once magnificent vessel.

IQ: As the affirmative aspect has been brought up, I thought it fair and important to ask you about another major affirmation throughout your work, namely, love and your manifold relation to your wife, Caryl, that many poems (say, from earlier "Eternity" to later "Combined Object") directly address. I believe your poems addressing love are an extremely powerful and original extension of "love poetry".

And beyond that, desire to integrate the woman, unhinged by the molds of male fantasy (while addressing the history-long male oppression), seems yet another principal aspect in your work. Am I correct in thinking so?

CE: Caryl and I rented a Volkswagen one Sunday in the spring of 1970, drove to Harriman State Park (New York) and ate LSD in the woods. Filled with that poison I began to shout for Hollie, my "new" Marie, another person I had chosen to desire as self-torture. We came back to the car at dusk, the parking-lot filled with picnicking Puerto Ricans. Caryl had her camera and we started taking pictures of each other over the back of the car. Once, looking through the lens I saw her—Caryl—not La Muerte, femme fatal, or housewife but an exasperated, sweating woman who was original! Not the image of

Woman, not superficial: fresh. This was the crucial moment in the early phase of our relationship. There is a more detailed account of this event in the last two pages of the poem "Coils" in my book *Coils*.

In the fall of 1973 in Paris, I began to regularly show Caryl poems I was working on and to ask her opinions about whether they made imaginative sense or not. For some forty years she has defined the meaning of "reader" and "editor" for me. As a sounding board, she has been invaluable. Her responses, mingling confirmation and resistance, have helped me see through superficial clarities as well as groundless obscurities. More specifically, she has rewritten passages (while in draft) or changed the direction of certain poems with a deft phrase and has taught me to allow another person to enter my creative space with rapport and love.

In the beginning, I was unsure as to whether I should share this activity with anyone. Being unsure meant that to share it with Caryl was a constant assault on my ego, putting my convictions on this or that to a test that often came down to whether what I had written made any kind of uncommon or even common sense. I think that this activity has been, and continues to me, one of the best things that has happened to me as a poet. I am confident that my body of work as it stands today would not have been realized without her key presence in my life.

Here is the dedication to my book *Juniper Fuse: Upper Paleolithic Imagination & the Construction of the Underworld*.

"Lespinasse, 1974: we carried our dinner outside to the stone table on the landing by the door to our second floor Bouyssou apartment. The farm was on a rise which slopped down through an apple orchard. When we sat down to eat, well before sunset, we had for entertainment an extraordinary sky. Clouds would come floating over the woods, spreading out over us. Puff collisions Mickey Mouse ears, shredding gargoyles, turrets, vales, mammoth apparitions densifying and disintegrating as they appeared. Many reminded us of the images we were trying to make out on the cave walls. To sit at that stone table—what an experience—to be in love there, at one of the most vital times in our many years together. Much of what happened—the 'event aspects'—during our first spring and summer in the Dordogne is now as dispersed as the clouds we used to watch—yet it billows in us, an inclusive cloud whose heart is ours."

From my first summer in Mexico, 1958, to the present, women have continually been one of the main focuses in my writing. I wrote about my mother in the poem "Hand," my complicated 1968 girlfriend Marie Benoit in "Diagonal," Adrienne Winograd for whom I left my first wife Barbara in 1966 in "The Golden String," Caryl Eshleman's childhood in "Sugar," and in the book What She Means (1978) there are many poems in which she appears. In 1981 I wrote a poem on the life of the Mexican painter Frida Kahlo, and in 1986 addressed my mythological heroine Ariadne in "Ariadne's Reunion." Some of my most ambitious poems have been on women painters like Nora Jaffe, Unica Zűrn, Nancy Spero, Joan Mitchell, Laura Solorzano, and Dorothea Tanning. And in my poems concerning the Upper Paleolithic caves I address a vulvaform I call "Our Lady of the Three-Pronged Devil," in "the mothers of Lascaux," a three-inch tall female statuette carved from mammoth tusk, "The Venus of Lespugue" in "Matrix, Blower," and the great Black Goddess in the cave of Le Combel that appears to be one of the first visions of The World Tree.

IQ: *There is a notion you bring up, here as well as elsewhere, that I thought might interest those yet unfamiliar with your work and practice in general: that of apprenticeship. 'Apprenticeship' might sound bizarre to many people interested in poetry today and I think it is something utterly unique that you have introduced into poetic practice. Could you briefly explain what poetic apprenticeship means to you?*

CE: The most complete response to this question is to be found in "A Translation Memoir" at the end of my translation of *The Complete Poetry of César Vallejo* (University of California Press, 2007). One afternoon in Kyoto in 1962 a friend, the American lithographer Will Petersen, mentioned that he had just visited a bonsai gardener who had completed his apprenticeship and was doing very interesting work. I had never thought of apprenticeship before, and I asked Will how old this man was. "He's in his early sixties," Will responded. Other than being moved that an artist would have such a long apprenticeship before doing his own work, I began to think that my difficulties in writing meaningful poems might be involved with my never having put myself through an apprenticeship. So I decided that instead of just trying to read the eighty-nine poems in César Vallejo's *Poemas humanos* which I had brought to Japan, maybe I should try to translate them as my apprenticeship to poetry. To do that meant an awesome commitment of psyche as well as time, especially since my Spanish was poor and self-taught, and Vallejo's poetry was very dense and complex. And in committing myself to such a project, was I simply evading the hard work of trying to find my way in poetry of my own? Or could I think of working on Vallejo as a way of working on myself?

In the afternoon I would ride my motorcycle downtown and work on translations in the Yorunomado coffee shop. Now, both in translating and working on poems of my own, I felt a weird resistance as if every attempt I made to advance was met by a force that pushed me back. I was as if through Vallejo I had made contact with a negative impaction in my being, a nebulous depth charge that I had been carrying around with me for many years. I also began to have violent and morbid fantasies that seemed provoked by the combination of translating and writing. I realized that I was struggling with a man as well as a text, and that this struggle was a matter of my becoming or failing to become a poet, and that this man I was struggling with was the old

Clayton who was resisting change. The old Clayton wanted to continue living in his white Presbyterian world of "light"—where man is associated with day/clarity/good and woman with night/opaqueness/bad. The darkness that was beginning to spread through my sensibility could be viewed as the breaking up of the belief in male supremacy that had generated much of that "light."

In an earlier response to one of your questions I mentioned a poem about struggling with a figure in this coffee shop. That poem is "The Book of Yorunomado."

The above should give you and your readers some idea of my apprenticeship, which also involved my conversations with Cid Corman, and once back in America in 1964, discovering the text of the Vallejo *Poemas humanos* that I was trying to translate had many errors and that the original manuscript was in the hands of Vallejo's French widow in Lima, Peru. In the spring of 1965, with my first wife Barbara pregnant, we left for Lima with a few hundred dollars. Once in Lima, I met Georgette Vallejo who refused to give me access to the worksheets upon which the various editions of the *Poemas humanos* were based. It was not until 1974, when I was living in Los Angeles with Caryl, that I was given access to the Moncloa edition of the book which for the first time reproduced Vallejo's worksheets.

IQ: *We have touched upon coming in terms with the Indiana background in your work, as well as what could be viewed as your maturity or gaining a fully formed voice as a poet (an involvement with what you call at one point "sacramental existence") that culminated in Juniper Fuse (around two decades in making), a work in many ways central not only to your body of work but, more generally, to the poetry of our time. There is yet another stage that you have been pursuing since and that you have elsewhere called "summational." As a reader, I first sensed it intensely in a poem called "The Tjurunga", where the lifelong work and involvement of*

the poet comes together as a constellation. Your new book, Penetralia,
struck me as central to this summational stage. Could you talk about this?
Further, sensing that the word "penetralia", must be important in many
ways, could you explain what it means to you in this book?

CE: I often open my 1955 Webster's New International Dictionary and
read a few pages at random. Doing so, one day a few years ago, I came
across the word "penetralia" which was defined as: "The innermost or
most private parts of thing or place, especially of a temple or palace."
A second definition followed: "Hidden things of secrets; privacy; sanc-
tuary; as the sacred penetralia of the home." Since I like words and
phrases for book titles that to my knowledge have not been used by
others as titles for poetry collections, I decided, then in my late 70s,
that "penetralia" would be an appropriate and unique title for what
might be my last collection of poetry, one that often ruminated on end
matters, or summational engagements. There are, of course, a number
of poems in this collection that do not directly do this, but the tone of
the writing, along with the end shadowings, justify such a title.

You mention a poem, "The Tjurunga," published in *Anticline*
(Black Widow Press, 2010) that I wrote was one of the two "soulend"
supports, along with the 1964 "Book of Yorunomado," holding the
rest of my poetry in place. In this later poem I propose a kind of com-
plex mobile (invoking the poet Robert Duncan's re-reading of that
mysterious Aranda ritual object) made up of the authors, mythologi-
cal figures and acts, whose shifting combinations undermined and
reoriented my life during my poetic apprenticeship in Kyoto, Japan, in
the early 1960s. At a remove of some forty-five years I saw these
forces as a kind of GPS (global positioning system) constantly "recal-
culating" as they closed and opened door after door. Thinking back
to Vallejo pointing at my gut (in "The Book of Yorunomado") and
indicating that I was to commit seppuku I was struck by the following

quotation from James Hillman's *Animal Presences*: "The theological message of the Siva-Ganesha, father-son pattern can be summarized in this way: submit that you may be saved, be destroyed that you may be made whole. The sacrificial violence is not the tragic conclusion but the necessary beginning of a passage into a new order… the God who breaks you makes you; destruction and creativity ultimately spring from the same source."

CLAYTON ESHLEMAN was born in Indianapolis, Indiana, June 1, 1935. He has a B.A. in Philosophy and an M.A.T. in English Literature from Indiana University. He has lived in Mexico, Japan, Taiwan, Korea, Peru, France, Czechoslovakia, and Hungary. He is presently Professor Emeritus, English Department, Eastern Michigan University. Since 1986 he has lived in Ypsilanti, Michigan with his wife Caryl who over the past forty years has been the primary reader and editor of his poetry and prose. His first collection of poetry, *Mexico & North*, was published in Kyoto, Japan in 1962.

From 1968 to 2004, Black Sparrow Press brought out thirteen collection of his poetry. In 2006, Black Widow Press became his main publisher and with *The Price of Experience* (2012) had brought out eight collections of his poetry, prose, and translations, including, in 2008, *The Grindstone of Rapport / A Clayton Eshleman Reader*. Wesleyan University Press has also published seven of his books, including *Juniper Fuse: Upper Paleolithic Imagination & the Construction of the Underworld* (2003), the first study of Ice Age cave art by a poet. Eshleman has published sixteen collections of translations, including *Watchfiends & Rack Screams* by Antonin Artaud (Exact Change, 1995), *The Complete Poetry of César Vallejo* with a Foreword by Mario Vargas Llosa (University of California Press, 2007), and *Aimé Césaire: The Collected Poetry* (co-translated with Annette Smith, University of California Press, 1983).

Clayton also founded and edited two of the most innovative poetry journals of the later part of the 20th century: *Caterpillar* (20 issues, 1967–1973) and *Sulfur* (46 issues, 1981–2000). Doubleday-Anchor published *A Caterpillar Anthology* in 1971 and Wesleyan in November 2015 published a 700-page *Sulfur Anthology*.

Among his recognitions and awards are a Guggenheim Fellowship in Poetry, 1978; The National Book Award in Translation, 1979; two grants from the NEA, 1979, 1981; three grants from the NEH, 1980,

1981, 1988; two Landon Translation Prizes from the Academy of American Poets, 1981, 2008; 13 NEA grants for *Sulfur* magazine, 1983–1996; The Alfonse X. Sabio Award for Excellence in Translation, San Diego State University, 2002; a Rockefeller Study Center residency in Bellagio, Italy, 2004, and a Hemmingway Translation Grant in 2015.

In 2014 Black Widow Press published *Clayton Eshleman / The Whole Art,* an anthology of essays on Eshleman's work over the decades, edited by Stuart Kendall. In the fall of 2015, Black Widow brought out *Clayton Eshleman / The Essential Poetry 1960–2015,* and in 2017 Wesleyan brought out a 950-page bilingual edition of *The Complete Poetry of Aimé Césaire,* co-translated with A. James Arnold. In 2017 Black Widow Press also published a new collection of poems by Eshleman called *Penetralia.*

His poetry has been featured in both volumes (1994 and 2013) of the *Norton Postmodern American Poetry.*

His website is www.claytoneshleman.com.

TITLES FROM BLACK WIDOW PRESS
TRANSLATION SERIES

A Life of Poems, Poems of a Life by Anna de Noailles. Edited and translated by Norman R. Shapiro. Introduction by Catherine Perry.

Approximate Man and Other Writings by Tristan Tzara. Translated and edited by Mary Ann Caws.

Art Poétique by Guillevic. Translated by Maureen Smith.

The Big Game by Benjamin Péret. Translated with an introduction by Marilyn Kallet.

Boris Vian Invents Boris Vian: A Boris Vian Reader. Edited and translated by Julia Older.

Capital of Pain by Paul Eluard. Translated by Mary Ann Caws, Patricia Terry, and Nancy Kline.

Chanson Dada: Selected Poems by Tristan Tzara. Translated with an introduction and essay by Lee Harwood.

Earthlight (Clair de Terre) by André Breton. Translated by Bill Zavatsky and Zack Rogow. (New and revised edition.)

Essential Poems and Prose of Jules Laforgue. Translated and edited by Patricia Terry.

Essential Poems and Writings of Joyce Mansour: A Bilingual Anthology. Translated with an introduction by Serge Gavronsky.

Essential Poems and Writings of Robert Desnos: A Bilingual Anthology. Edited with an introduction and essay by Mary Ann Caws.

Eye Seas (Les Ziaux) by Raymond Queneau. Translated with an introduction by Daniela Hurezanu and Stephen Kessler.

Fables in a Modern Key by Pierre Coran. Translated by Norman R. Shapiro. Full-color illustrations by Olga Pastuchiv.

Fables of Town & Country by Pierre Coran. Translated by Norman R. Shapiro. Full-color illustrations by Olga Pastuchiv.

Forbidden Pleasures: New Selected Poems 1924–1949 by Luis Cernuda. Translated by Stephen Kessler.

Furor and Mystery & Other Writings by René Char. Translated by Mary Ann Caws and Nancy Kline.

The Gentle Genius of Cécile Périn: Selected Poems (1906–1956). Edited and translated by Norman R. Shapiro.

Guarding the Air: Selected Poems of Gunnar Harding. Translated and edited by Roger Greenwald.

Howls & Growls: French Poems to Bark By. Translated by Norman R. Shapiro; illustrated by Olga K. Pastuchiv.

I Have Invented Nothing: Selected Poems by Jean-Pierre Rosnay. Translated by J. Kates.

In Praise of Sleep: Selected Poems of Lucian Blaga Translated with an introduction by Andrei Codrescu.

The Inventor of Love & Other Writings by Gherasim Luca. Translated by Julian & Laura Semilian. Introduction by Andrei Codrescu. Essay by Petre Răileanu.

Jules Supervielle: Selected Prose and Poetry. Translated by Nancy Kline & Patricia Terry.

La Fontaine's Bawdy by Jean de La Fontaine. Translated with an introduction by Norman R. Shapiro.

Last Love Poems of Paul Eluard. Translated with an introduction by Marilyn Kallet.

Love, Poetry (L'amour la poésie) by Paul Eluard. Translated with an essay by Stuart Kendall.

Pierre Reverdy: Poems, Early to Late. Translated by Mary Ann Caws and Patricia Terry.

Poems of André Breton: A Bilingual Anthology. Translated with essays by Jean-Pierre Cauvin and Mary Ann Caws.

Poems of A.O. Barnabooth by Valery Larbaud. Translated by Ron Padgett and Bill Zavatsky.

Poems of Consummation by Vicente Aleixandre. Translated by Stephen Kessler.

Préversities: A Jacques Prévert Sampler. Translated and edited by Norman R. Shapiro.

RhymAmusings (AmuseRimes) by Pierre Coran. Translated by Norman R. Shapiro.

The Sea and Other Poems by Guillevic. Translated by Patricia Terry. Introduction by Monique Chefdor.

Through Naked Branches by Tarjei Vesaas. Translated, edited, and introduced by Roger Greenwald.

To Speak, to Tell You? Poems by Sabine Sicaud. Translated by Norman R. Shapiro. Introduction and notes by Odile Ayral-Clause.

MODERN POETRY SERIES

BARNSTONE, WILLIS.
ABC of Translation
African Bestiary (forthcoming)

BRINKS, DAVE.
The Caveat Onus
The Secret Brain: Selected Poems 1995–2012

CESEREANU, RUXANDRA.
Crusader-Woman. Translated by Adam J. Sorkin.
    Introduction by Andrei Codrescu.
Forgiven Submarine by Ruxandra Cesereanu
    and Andrei Codrescu.

ESHLEMAN, CLAYTON.
An Alchemist with One Eye on Fire
Anticline
Archaic Design
Clayton Eshleman / The Essential Poetry: 1960–2015
Grindstone of Rapport: A Clayton Eshleman Reader
Penetralia
Pollen Aria
The Price of Experience
Endure: Poems by Bei Dao. Translated by
    Clayton Eshleman and Lucas Klein.
Curdled Skulls: Poems of Bernard Bador. Translated
    by Bernard Bador with Clayton Eshleman.

JORIS, PIERRE.
Barzakh (Poems 2000–2012)
Exile Is My Trade: A Habib Tengour Reader

KALLET, MARILYN.
How Our Bodies Learned
The Love That Moves Me
Packing Light: New and Selected Poems
Disenchanted City (La ville désenchantée)
    by Chantal Bizzini. Translated by J. Bradford
    Anderson, Darren Jackson, and Marilyn Kallet.

KELLY, ROBERT.
Fire Exit
The Hexagon

KESSLER, STEPHEN.
Garage Elegies

LAVENDER, BILL.
Memory Wing

LEVINSON, HELLER.
from stone this running
LinguaQuake
Tenebraed
Un-
Wrack Lariat

OLSON, JOHN.
Backscatter: New and Selected Poems
Dada Budapest
Larynx Galaxy

OSUNDARE, NIYI.
City Without People: The Katrina Poems

ROBERTSON, MEBANE.
An American Unconscious
Signal from Draco: New and Selected Poems

ROTHENBERG, JEROME.
Concealments and Caprichos
Eye of Witness: A Jerome Rothenberg Reader.
    Edited with commentaries by Heriberto Yepez
    & Jerome Rothenberg.
The President of Desolation & Other Poems

SAÏD, AMINA.
The Present Tense of the World: Poems 2000–2009.
    Translated with an introduction by
    Marilyn Hacker.

SHIVANI, ANIS.
Soraya (Sonnets)

WARD, JERRY W., JR.
Fractal Song

ANTHOLOGIES / BIOGRAPHIES

*Barbaric Vast & Wild: A Gathering of Outside and
Subterranean Poetry (Poems for the Millennium,
vol. 5).* Editors: Jerome Rothenberg and
John Bloomberg-Rissman

Clayton Eshleman: The Whole Art by Stuart Kendall

Revolution of the Mind: The Life of André Breton
by Mark Polizzotti

WWW.BLACKWIDOWPRESS.COM